Organizational Transitions

Second Edition

Organizational Transitions

Managing Complex Change

Richard Beckhard
Richard Beckhard Associates

Reuben T. Harris
The Tom Peters Group

Addison-Wesley Publishing Company
Reading, Massachusetts • Menlo Park, California • Don Mills, Ontario • Wokingham, England • Amsterdam • Sydney • Singapore • Tokyo • Madrid • Bogotá • Santiago • San Juan

This book is in the Addison-Wesley Series on Organization Development.
Editors: Edgar H. Schein, Richard Beckhard

Other titles in the series:

Organization Development:
A Normative View
W. Warner Burke

Team Building:
Issues and Alternatives, Second Edition
William G. Dyer

The Technology Connection:
Strategy and Change in the Information Age
Marc S. Gerstein

Stream Analysis:
A Powerful Way to Diagnose and Manage Organizational Change
Jerry I. Porras

Process Consultation Volume II:
Lessons for Managers and Consultants
Edgar H. Schein

Managing Conflict:
Interpersonal Dialogue and Third-Party Roles,
Second Edition
Richard E. Walton

Library of Congress Cataloging-in-Publication Data

Beckhard, Richard, 1918–
Organizational transitions.

(Addison-Wesley series on organization development)
1. Organizational change. I. Harris, Reuben T.
II. Title. III. Series.
HD58.8.B4 1987 658.4'06 86–25863
ISBN 0–201–10887–9

EFGHIJ–BA–89

Foreword

The Addison-Wesley Series on Organization Development originated in the late 1960s when a number of us recognized that the rapidly growing field of "OD" was not well understood or well defined. We also recognized that there was no one OD philosophy, and hence one could not at that time write a textbook on the theory and practice of OD, but one could make clear what various practitioners were doing under that label. So the original six books by Beckhard, Bennis, Blake and Mouton, Lawrence and Lorsch, Schein, and Walton launched what has since become a continuing enterprise. The essence of this enterprise was to let different authors speak for themselves instead of trying to summarize under one umbrella what was obviously a rapidly growing and highly diverse field.

By 1981 the series included nineteen titles, having added books by Beckhard and Harris, Cohen and Gadon, Davis, Dyer, Galbraith, Hackman and Oldham, Heenan and Perlmutter, Kotter, Lawler, Nadler, Roeber, Schein, and Steele. This proliferation reflected what had happened to the field of OD. It was growing by leaps and bounds, and it was expanding into all kinds of organizational areas and technologies of intervention. By this time many textbooks existed as well that tried to capture the core concepts of the field, but we felt that diversity and innovation were still the more salient aspects of OD today.

The present series is an attempt both to recapture some basics and to honor the growing diversity. So we have begun a series of revisions of some of the original books and have added a set of new authors or old authors with new content. Our hope is to capture the spirit of inquiry and innovation that has always been the hallmark of organization development and to launch with these books a new wave of insights into the forever tricky problem of how to change and improve organizations.

We are grateful that Addison-Wesley has chosen to continue the series and are also grateful to the many reviewers who have helped us and the authors in the preparation of the current series of books.

Cambridge, Massachusetts Edgar H. Schein
New York, New York Richard Beckhard

Preface

When we wrote the first edition of this book, managing change had become a matter of increasing concern for executive managements. At that time there was a body of knowledge and technology, developed over the previous fifteen years, that was understood by academicians, applied by "organization development practitioners," and generally not understood by organizational managements. Our intention was to try, in some way, to help make that knowledge and technology available to organization leaders in their management of complexity.

What was an abstract matter of concern to organization management a decade ago is now everyday management practice. Given the rash of takeovers, mergers, changes in mission, and shifts in strategic orientation from technology-driven to market-driven, the management of these complex changes has become a central executive management agenda. In addition, the *dilemma* of achieving or managing change while maintaining enough stability to continue to do whatever the organization is supposed to do provides new challenges and new requirements for executive management.

Our first edition focused on the change process and did not pay much attention to the existence of this "change–stability" dilemma. How do you simultaneously "manufacture refrigerators and, on the other hand, plan their obsolescence in order to maintain competitive advantage?" How do you do this with the same work force and the same management group? "How do you keep the store running profitably while you're converting it into a supermarket?"

These types of questions illustrate a generic issue confronting most managements today. In this revised edition, we look at the issues of managing change and managing complexity from the point of view of this dilemma, and more specifically, from the perspective of the executive management that faces the problem.

Therefore, we're paying attention to issues such as organization culture. Given a merger, let's say, of Procter & Gamble and Richardson-Vicks—giant companies—what will be the emerging culture? What will be the ways of work? The leadership style? The ground rules? The reward systems? The attitudes toward people? Should the new organization be two separate organizations under an umbrella, or should they be truly "merged"? How does one increase, or even maintain, productivity, creativity, or innovation (if that's desired)? With the availability and the potential competitive advantage of effective use of information technology and telecommunications for decision making, customer service, worldwide communications, revised working methods, and so on, how do we (a) decide how the work should be organized in relation to these new technologies, and (b) deal with the human organization as we convert from one way of operating to a different one?

This edition attempts to take into account the changing environment and to provide for the reader–practitioner a contemporary look at how existing knowledge and technology can be usefully applied. We will examine briefly the basic classes of problems or forces making demands on the organization leader. We will look at the environment and the demand systems, and discuss how some techniques, such as open-systems planning, can help executive management establish priorities and practices to balance stability and change. We will study various organizational structures and their implications for managerial strategies. We will examine the change process in terms of a *future state*—the condition when the change has occurred; the *present state*—

the period of planning and initiating the desired change; and the *transition state*—the getting from here to there. We will assess the major decisions in determining activities and priorities, and view the choices involved in developing an appropriate system to manage the transition. We will examine strategies for securing commitment to change among the members of an organization—a necessity in order for the desired change to occur. Finally, we will look a little deeper at some of the general issues related to managing change and complexity.

Since 1977, we've learned more about what it takes to effectively manage the dilemma of stability versus change. We hope to leave the reader with some guidelines that can be useful and readily applied as he or she manages this increasingly central issue in organizations.

We are grateful to all of those who have helped us in our learning and in the development of this book. We are particularly grateful to our clients and organizations with whom we have worked who have provided the live material from which we could draw. We are also grateful to Ed Schein for his continued collaboration, interest, and his most appreciated critical eye.

Thanks also to Sherry Masterson and Linda Pollock, who typed and retyped the manuscript.

Last, but certainly not least, we are grateful to our families, those loved ones who lost the competitive battle for our time while we were preparing this book.

Contents

Organizational Transitions

1

Managing Complex Change

Even the Future Ain't What It Was

The world in which organizations exist, and will be operating for the rest of this century, is continuously in change: change in relationships among nations, institutions, business partners, and organizations; change in the makeup of the "haves" and "have nots"; change in dominant values and norms governing society and our institutions; change in the character and culture of business or wealth-producing organizations; change in how work is done; change in priorities about how we spend our time and our lives.

In such a world, a core dilemma for executives and leaders is how to maintain stability in their organizations and, at the same time, provide creative adaptation to outside forces; stimulate innovation; and change assumptions, technology, working methods, roles, and relationships, and the culture of the organization itself.

In the first edition of this book, we undertook to identify some of the major trends of the late 1970s–early 1980s that we felt would profoundly affect organizational stability and change.

We were generally correct, but incorrect on some of our specific predictions.

We said the environment would remain complex — a safe bet. We said that "values will play an increasingly important part in environmental pressures." Actually, that role has leveled out, not increased. We said governmental control would increase; it has decreased in many of the First World countries, particularly the United States and the United Kingdom. We said that employees would continue to have high expectations on joining a firm — still a defensible prediction.

We said that many middle managers would be changing priorities about work and leisure. True: the readiness for rethinking lifestyles has made it a lot easier for companies to accomplish massive layoffs, early retirements, "golden handshakes," and "golden parachutes."

We said there would be a leveling out of the impact of new technology. How wrong we were! This influence is increasing exponentially and offers both problems and challenges unanticipated by management and by those who wrote about it ten years ago.

We said that bottom level-entry employees would have lower expectations. The evidence is not in — and the problem is not a priority anymore.

Challenges

In this edition we want to look first at the challenges facing those who would manage complex institutional change and the dilemma of balancing change and stability. The key issues we pose are:

1. Changing the Shape of Organizations

In response to increased worldwide competition, dramatic growth of technology, and rapidly expanding patterns of takeovers, mergers, and restructuring, many organizations are having to transform their own shape. To use an analogy, if one were to increase the weight of a deer by several hundred pounds, one would have to shorten its legs in order for it to bear the additional weight. Organizations today have the same challenge. What is the appropriate shape for them to meet the increasing demand to grow, and best survive the expansion?

2. Changes in the Mission or "Reason To Be."

For the same reasons as above, many of the same organizations are having to reexamine their raison d'être, or reason to be, and to develop strategies for establishing or broadening a niche for themselves.

3. Changes in Ways of Doing Business

Due to increased pressures from the environment or shifts in the priorities of the organization's leadership, changes in structure, strategy, and management style are increasingly demanded.

4. Changes in Ownership

Providing more employee ownership, different kinds of profit sharing, and more psychological as well as economic ownership in an enterprise is a change requiring careful management.

5. Downsizing

For twenty-five years the general pattern for organizations in both the public and private sectors has been growth. Today, for many organizations the pattern is downsizing, working leaner and smarter, and reducing growth in order to ensure survival and further growth later.

6. Changes in the Culture of the Organization

Particularly due to mergers, takeovers, and combinations of businesses, the management of two cultures and creation of a third combined one are issues central to an organization's excellence and, in fact, its survival.

Changing Shape

A historian of organizations would note that a distinguishing characteristic of the early 1980s in American, and now British, business is the massive number of takeovers and mergers among large enterprises. The basic assumption that Fortune 500–type companies are immune to "takeovers" has been overridden by experience. We find every day that some large company has succumbed to friendly or unfriendly takeovers. Merger is sometimes the only option for economic survival, and it is becoming increasingly common. In addition to the large companies, hundreds of small companies are going the same route.

If we add to this condition the explosion of competition from Japan, West Germany, and, in some cases, Third World countries, we see that enterprise managers are now faced with a need to examine the basic *shape* of their organizations.

A third major force acting on business is new technology, particularly information technology and the opportunities it offers for gaining a competitive advantage and for reexamining the nature of the business enterprise.

Not very long ago, anyone would have been able to tell you that a bank is a different type of institution from an insurance company and that neither of these are the same as an investment company. Today it is rare to think of these enterprises as separate and distinct; they all call themselves financial service companies. And who are they? Well, in addition to banks such as Citibank and investment organizations such as Merrill Lynch and American Express, we find Sears and other such institutions becoming financial service companies. The nature of the industry has changed, and so have its activities and participants. One can predict that within a very few years, members of the financial industry will no longer define themselves as financial service companies, but as "information companies," since the mobility and availability of information will be the factors that provide competitive quality difference. Since consumers today are more and more buying for quality rather than price, financial service companies who wish to remain in the race will be relying ever more on creative use of information and an orientation toward service — a major change from what we used to think of as banking, for example.

In a perhaps less dramatic but equally potent transformational change, an organization such as Eastman Kodak, which for many, many years purchased all the supplies it needed to manufacture film and operated as a self-contained, highly centralized production organization, is now transformed into a market-driven organization with buy–make decisions being the normal course of events. It's not just a new way of doing business; it's a change in the shape of the beast, change in the kinds of products and businesses.

Changes in Mission

Although all of the categories listed here overlap slightly, it is helpful to differentiate them in thinking about change management. For example, if we think of the word "mission" as "reason to be," then the question might be, for a company such as Exxon, what is its reason to be? Is it an oil company? An energy company? A financial conglomerate? The way Exxon's leadership answers this question carries tremendous implications for the organization, such as priorities for the allocation of financial resources.

Traditionally, in a medical school producing physicians is the core "reason to be." But in today's world, the main purpose may be to provide physicians who can function in the community in which the school is located; the real mission is to *provide services* to that community. Or it may be that the mission is to find the cure for cancer through the school's research activities. Which role a school sees for itself is defined by its stewards, and the decision controls the organizational structure, budget priorities, and so on.

In a youth organization such as the Boy Scouts or Girl Scouts, the mission may change from providing educational and citizenship activities for young people to mobilizing them to take stands on social issues.

Changes in Ways of Doing Business

Because of all the current outside forces, organization leaders have had to become more specifically differentiated in how they're doing business. This new focus may take the form of redefining one's strategy for the business. For example, is the firm to be directed as a *portfolio* business, in which the subparts are considered investments to be bought or sold by the center? Or perhaps the strategy is to be one of a *conglomerate,* in which the center seeks vertical and lateral integration; buys management rather than assets; and allows relatively independent entities to produce profits jointly and to see themselves as part of one large institution, with such benefits are such things as centralized buying and large financial resources. A third, familiar alternative is *executive* management, a style in which the decisions move upward to a highly centralized leadership group.

Strategic Management

Emerging more and more is the concept of *strategic management,* in which the individual business entities each respond to a central 'directorate' whose function it is to plan the general corporate strategy. The units operate not only as profit centers but also as relatively autonomous organizations, relating to the center with a minimal need for supervision or direction. In other words, they manage their own objectives with goals, targets, and periodic but not too frequent progress reports to the center. If the leadership changes the strategy of an organization from, say, executive management to strategic management, the implications for structure, ways of work, and rewards are significant.

Also, one may decide to change the organization's priorities. Most excellent organizations are recognizing that, in today's world, quality and service are increasingly important for effectiveness. Which of two airlines one flies has much more to do with service and customer orientation than with whether airplane one is different from airplane two. The decision about a hotel is made by a client after he or she arrives, depending upon the treatment given by the reception clerks and the bellboys.

Within organizations as well, more and more the parts of the organization are "customers" for each other. This change in ways of doing business to more effective internal support and interrelationship can be a strong competitive factor. McDonald's does not enjoy the position it has in the marketplace entirely because of the quality of its hamburgers. Changes in priorities for doing business have implications for changes in structure. For example, when adding major hospital patient care to clinical care became the number one priority in a major teaching hospital, the organization of separate functions such as nursing and nutrition needed to be reexamined in customer terms. Teams of staff members, including nurses and dieticians, were assigned to geographic areas of the hospital so that they could combine their resources to optimize patient care. This shift brought great changes in structure, reporting lines, and reward systems.

Changes in Ownership

What makes Delta Airlines such an effective enterprise? Well, part of it is efficiency, and the priority service orientation.

A large part of it has to do with the quality of the relationship between personnel and the customer.

The employees of Delta own, both literally and psychologically, significant amounts of stock. We find today that a way of resolving the labor unrest in organizations such as Eastern Airlines may well be a change in ownership, with more employee ownership. The experimental Saturn program, in which General Motors is engaged at this writing, is based on the assumption that everyone owning the problems and challenges is essential to provide the innovation and quality necessary to produce a car, given American labor costs, that will be competitive with the rest of the world.

Downsizing

Because of advances in technological innovation, robotics, and information technology, considerable reductions in staff will be necessary for continued efficiency. Maintaining the quality of the organization while reducing the numbers of people who are doing the work is a real challenge that is claiming a lot of executive attention today.

Changes in Culture

The word "culture," a popular word these days, is distinct from organizational *climate*, which is a measure of the morale or happiness of a staff at any particular time. What we mean by *culture* is that set of artifacts, beliefs, values, norms, and ground rules that defines and significantly influences how the organization operates. Given the large number of takeovers and mergers today, one of the most common change management issues is the management of two cultures — the culture of the acquiring company and that of the company that's taken over. This issue can be critical in small family-owned firms, where the cultures of the family and the firm have to be mediated by the founder or leader of each in order to ensure the organization's survival and its competitive position.

Conditions for Effective Management of Change

To manage these issues, organization leaders need to establish the following:

- a vision of what the institution should look like, and direction toward that vision.
- a clear sense of the organization's identity (reason to be).
- a clear sense of the organization's interdependency with its outside environment. The organizational system consists of both the formal organization and those parts of the environment that constantly affect it, such as competitors or technology.
- clear and reachable *scenarios* (not objectives, but descriptions of end states that also define what the organization should look like at an intermediate point). Scenarios should be clear enough to provide the basis for developing strategic plans, including, contingency choices.
- flexible enough organizational structures to manage optimally the types of work required, production, innovation, business strategies, market intelligence, information management, people management, and creative financial planning.
- effective use of advanced technology. Managers, not technicians, should determine office technology, production, and telecommunication applications.
- reward systems that equally reflect organization priorities, values, and norms and individual needs for dignity and growth.

Leadership Requirements

To create and sustain such patterns, executives and managers need both skills and understanding in areas that were not a priority ten years ago. They must have a good grasp of the changing nature of work in the information age; telecommunications technology and its potential role for the organization; the nature of culture and what it takes to change it; the significant role of values in an organization's life; the general sociopolitical nature of the world; impacts of currencies and East–West/North–South issues; and finally (the subject of this book), the technology and concepts of managing effective change and of balancing stability and change.

In Chapter 2 we will look at those factors in the organizational system (formal organization and environment) that make demands on the leadership of the organization and affect decisions concerning change.

In Chapter 3 we will step back to take a longer-lensed look at organizations in their entirety, and discuss briefly some characteristics of effectiveness in any organization.

Chapter 4 starts a specific look at the change process. We will study how one defines a need for change, assess the role of the change manager, and survey the beginnings of developing a strategy and action plan in the change situation.

In Chapter 5 we look at the future state — the post-change goal.

Chapter 6 will focus on the present situation in the context of the anticipated future state.

Chapter 7 examines the transition state — the getting from here to there.

In Chapter 8 we present a more extensive case study of how one organization managed a complex change.

In Chapter 9 we change our focus from managing the actual work of a change to getting the commitment of the people who must carry it out. We discuss commitment planning and strategies for securing it.

Finally, in Chapter 10, we take a very brief look at what the future might hold for us.

Now for a look at the organizational system.

2

The Demand System

Forces in the Environment

Anyone in a leadership position in a complex organization knows viscerally that the formal organization or hierarchy only partially represents it. The true picture includes the formal organization; relevant "outside" domains such as competitors, regulators, and suppliers; and societal issues such as environmentalism, women's rights, and age discrimination; global location, as influenced by such factors as competing countries and differing value systems; and last but not least, the explosion of technology — particularly communications technology.

Given this myriad of constituencies making demands on the leadership, the policies, decisions, and actions of the organization leadership become those of *managing* these varied demands from both outside and inside the organizational system.

Issues of control, procedures, and rewards are very different in this type of world from those in an organization where power rests solely in the hierarchy, and the rewards and punishments available ensure control of the organization's behavior by its leaders.

Let us look briefly at some of these classes of demands and their implications for managing both change and stability.

Multiple Constituencies

Organizations have traditionally answered to a primary constituency — stockholders in a business, patients and the community in a hospital. Management today must think in terms of a number of constituents: institutions, such as labor unions, professional associations, or governments; regulations and policies; societal values; and technological innovations.

Technological Innovations

With the incredible increase in sophistication of information technology, it is now both possible and affordable to use technical and computer assistance to perform many of life's tasks. One can order groceries, make banking transactions, send Christmas cards, retrieve books from the "library," and access the world's information without ever leaving the living room, or wherever the terminal is located.

In the workplace, it is practical to be able to write letters on a word processor, to design a building across the ocean through telecommunications, to have instant or continuous contact with branches of a company through closed-circuit video, and to have continuous worldwide intraorganization communication through your own satellite. These technologies, by giving access to information in seconds rather than weeks, have altered the actual shape and character of many organizations. For example, most financial services institutions that used to be thought of as separate industries — banking, insurance, investment — are now providing all these services, and are recognizing that basically they are not money-related institutions but *information*-related institutions. The worldwide bank that can process a loan twice as fast because of its integrated "common systems" computer network has a significant competitive advantage. Similarly, every sales representative who carries a portable computer to handle paperwork can free up a third more time in the field for selling. If a supplier puts a terminal in the customer's ordering department, the ordering and delivery of goods is sped up by a factor of 4 or 5.

To respond to this increasing rate of change and complexity, the manager must think in terms very different from those traditionally used to "manage an organization."

Changing Values

Concurrent with the technology explosion is a trend in the work force toward more autonomy, more flexibility, more demand for work to be meaningful, and less "organization loyalty." Most entering employees today are taking a *job* or a position — not committing to a career with the organization they join. This tendency means that managements must think differently about a "temporary" and changing work force. It also means that the organizational structures and ways of work must live in some tension between stability and change.

Regulations and Constraints

As people live longer, become more aware of the need to protect life on the planet, and become more health-conscious, governments increase environmental standards on all sorts of products, thus producing constraints on the freedom of the business to control its own destiny. Managements must have a sophisticated intelligence network available to monitor a whole variety of these constraints, and must be prepared for quick adaptations to them.

Other Institutions

The impact of other institutions on management such as labor unions, competitors, suppliers, and consumer groups continues to be potent, but its centrality has been overtaken by the other forces we have mentioned. Nevertheless, management must still have a flexible style to react creatively to pressures from these traditional sources.

The Nature of Tasks

In the earlier edition of this book we talked about the increasing complexity of the tasks in an organization. In the intervening ten years the problem has changed from increasing *com-*

plexity of tasks to *new types of tasks.* With the advent of sophisticated hardware and software, increased automation, robots, and so on, the employee who used to be a manual laborer is now a decision maker. He or she is watching dials and digital readouts, looking for deviations from a standard of performance, and making decisions about significant actions for the machines to take. This change of responsibility requires much more than just "retraining." It requires reconceptualizing the nature of work; moving toward using the head more than the hands — making judgments never before demanded; and dealing with the tension of "being responsible." This is not an evolutionary transformation in the way work is done; it is revolutionary. It means that managements must define and manage the cultural and behavioral changes necessary for an organization to work in this new environment.

Open-Systems Planning

In recent years the emergence of an increasing constellation of demands from environments surrounding organizations has motivated some organizational leaders to search aggressively for, develop, and experiment with specific processes for their systemwide planning. One such institutional planning process is the seven-phase *open-systems planning*. Basically, it is a process of analyzing a situation, identifying the kind of social and technical environment necessary to operate effectively, and developing a strategy for getting there. In brief, the steps are:

1. Determine the "core mission" of the organization.
2. Map the demand system.
3. Map the current response system.
4. Project the probable demand system, given no change in organization impact.
5. Identify the desired state.
6. List activities necessary to achieve the desired state.
7. Define cost-effective options.

The entire process of open-systems planning might be called a diagnostic process of preplanning. We will briefly describe what each phase involves and how it is used.

Core Mission. An organization's *mission* is different from organizational *objectives.* An organization's mission is its reason for being; an organization's objectives are its goals, the states it wants to achieve. Organizational leaders tend to take the organization's mission for granted. For example, business organizational leaders might say, "Our mission is to maximize profits for the shareholders"; directors of a medical school might say, "Our mission is to train doctors," or "Our mission is to do biomedical research, furthering knowledge and providing opportunities for doctors to be trained in the most advanced technology."

Based on the statements above, one could define the organizational mission of the business enterprise as: (1) to maximize return of investment to *shareholders;* (2) to optimize return on investment; (3) to provide more useful products to society; and (4) to provide employment. Or, one could say that the core mission of the medical school is: (1) to do biomedical research; (2) to train doctors; and (3) to provide, through its teaching hospitals, the specialty care not available in other delivery settings.

In one sense, an organizational mission is the sum of all "reasons to be." The problem is that a core mission cannot be all of them equally; it must set priorities. In a complex organization with a variety of conflicting demands for allocation of resources, programs or investment priorities, and distribution of profits or other "goodies," the executive management must make the often painful choice of which "mission" is number one — the *core mission.* If the core mission is to maximize return to shareholders, that maximization defines and constrains many managerial plans and actions. If, on the other hand, the core mission is to provide employment, the implications for managerial strategy and actions are quite different.

In a simple organization, it does not matter very much to what degree one differentiates the various mission statements. For example, suppose that Alice Smith's hobby is pottery; her mission at this point is to make ceramic pieces for her own enjoyment. After a while, she starts to give away these objects to friends. One of them says, "Look, these are quite marketable. If you could make more of them, I think we could open a store to sell them, and you could have the fun of making them while getting some money as well. If you make them, I will market them." We now have the beginnings of a complex organization, and the mission becomes a little more clouded. Is the "core reason for being" to have fun, to make money, or what? If a store that originally ordered ten of these pieces now orders a thousand, different kinds of machinery and production processes will be required. What now becomes the mission and what implications grow out of the changed conditions? Alice now has to make significant personal choices; does she want to "go into business," or keep her hobby?

All sorts of operational decisions grow out of setting priorities. Managers of economic enterprises are very familiar with the conflict between the missions of growth and maximizing short-term profits. One cannot have it both ways, so all sorts of trade-offs must be made, based on some manager's or group of managers' personal judgment as to which is the more important mission. Similarly, in the case of the medical school with three missions, the way the school actually operates, the type of faculty recruited, budget allocations, the relationship of teaching to research, and so forth all depend on how the leadership of the institution sees the primary mission: teaching doctors, conducting biomedical research and science, or delivering patient care.

One can look at schools or economic organizations or governments around the world and see clear differences based on the leaders' definition of the core mission. The point is that although it may seem obvious or to be busywork, top management must invest the energy in reaching consensus on priorities and establishing a clear core mission.

Determining the core mission requires an analysis of the character of the markets — the needs of owners, employees, and consumers regarding the organization. In three case examples later in the chapter, we describe how different executive managements chose a core mission and put it into practice. Two points should be emphasized:

1. The operable decision about core mission is the one that the top management of the organization uses to guide its priori-

ties in goal setting, resource allocation, and other decisions. It is always, in the final analysis, a personal judgment of one or a few key executives.

2. It is important — often crucial — that the key managing executives of the organization be in consensus about the mission. If they are not, their behavior can result in mixed commitment to organization goal priorities.

Mapping the Demand System. At any given time, there are a number of different groups and institutions making demands on an organization's leaders. Executive management must sort these demands in terms of the organization's mission and goal priorities, and weigh their urgency.

In putting these demands in perspective and in relationship to one another, it is helpful to make a map of the various institutions or groups and to identify their specific demands. A technique called "environmental mapping" has been developed to facilitate this process. First, management develops a visual chart listing all of the groups, institutions, or conditions (the jargon word is "domains") that are saying to the organization, "We want you to . . . !" Next, five to ten of the most relevant "domains" are selected, and a list of their specific demands is developed. For example, the trade unions might demand higher wages, salaries, and benefits for their members; young employees might want a different kind of socialization process and increased opportunities for promotion; environmentalists might want the organization to invest significant sums of capital to reduce pollution from its operations or plants; senior management might want a revision of compensation systems and work organization; the government of a country may want the organization's leaders to emphasize employment rather than profit; and the shareholders may demand an increased short-run return on investment.

After mapping the demand system, the next step is to identify current organizational responses to these demands.

Current Response System. Now the organization's current response to each of the demands identified in the previous phase is specified. For example, given demands from the government, women and minorities employees, and citizens' groups for the organization to increase its affirmative action activity, the organization can respond in a variety of ways. One option is to "do as little as you can, just enough to stay out of jail." Another is to "do what the others do" — the average for the industry or community. A third is to take an active posture, such as setting improvement targets and committing resources for training and recruitment activities. Most organizations give lip service to this active response pattern, but their practice is usually quite different.

Whichever response is adopted, everyone at the top management level must agree to it. The process of working toward consensus also provides opportunities for assessing the consequences of different responses. For example, an organization's decision to minimize its commitment to affirmative action may lead to legal suits, loss of government contracts, or both. Therefore, this response pattern is a relatively uneconomic and "unsocial" one to maintain.

Projected Demand System. The next step in the process is for management to make a three- or four-year projection of the current demands, assuming that the organization were to do nothing significant in response in the interim. For example, is consumerism likely to be stronger, weaker, or about the same three years from now? Is Ralph Nader's movement likely to have more, less, or the same impact on the organization's policies and practices as it does now? Laid against the current response system, this type of projection increases the clarity of likely consequences of the current response plan.

Desired State. The next step is to define what the organization would like in three or four years. For example, leaders of a private enterprise might want the government to be giving more support to private industry through increased tax relief. They might also hope for their organization to be regarded as the most desirable place to work by significant numbers of top college graduates. In short, the map of the desired state provides some relatively clear and specific goals and the basis for beginning to identify a set of actions for moving toward a more desirable condition.

Activity Planning. Here the process is to identify those types of activities, organizational forms, investments, and projects that would be necessary to achieve the desired state.

Assessing Cost-Effectiveness. This is an analysis of the social and economic costs of the action alternatives identified in the previous step; it is an important step in strategic planning.

Case Illustrations of Open-Systems Planning

Case 1: A New Manufacturing Plant. A company making and selling a variety of consumer products was building a new plant designed to produce a very popular product for which increased manufacturing capacity was needed. Each manufacturing plant of the parent company was a cost center, making a product according to requirements from the profit-center marketing organizations. Orders to both plant and distribution were controlled by the marketing organization.

This new plant was to produce "glup," using a technology already highly developed and in practice in other plants producing the same product. Raw material came in a powdered form into an assembly line from a warehouse, was poured into a big funnellike machine that mixed it with some other materials, and was produced as an output product, also in powdered form. Through a relatively highly automated process, this finished product was put in boxes or bottles, which were then packed, sealed, stacked, and prepared for shipment.

In other plants using this technology, the production line required five operators, plus a maintenance person available to handle any mechanical problems with the equipment, as shutdowns were extremely costly. A foreman supervised the five operators and machine-maintenance person.

The new plant was to be built in a small midwestern town and would have a major impact on the community, providing significant employment and tax revenue. Based on previous experiments using open-systems concepts to start up plants, management decided that this plant would be socially and technically designed from the outset. A task force composed of the plant manager, the engineers building the plant, behavioral science-oriented staff, operations research and information systems people, and significant group leaders from the plant was named a design team and given wide latitude for innovation.

First, the task force examined the core mission of the new plant. What was to be the nature of this plant? All similar plants in the company had as their core mission the producing of a high-quality, optimum-cost product as needed by the company. This design team said no; the core mission of the new plant was to be in the "glup" business. Therefore, rather than being a cost center producing a product, the new plant would need very different linkages with the environment around it, including headquarters management, distribution, and so on. For example, under the old system, the inventories held by a plant could become very expensive, depending on the whims of the marketplace. Because the plant was not measured as a cost center alone, it was possible to operate differently to produce optimum effectiveness. For example, the plant management and the brand management would be looking together at how to optimize such things as inventories.

From this core mission, the design team reviewed the traditional demands on technology and personnel: having as tight a work force as possible, five operators to a shift. The team studied demands in the engineering area for having full-time technicians at each machine, demands on the system for adequate control over ordering supplies and regulating the work flow, and the current operating procedures of other plants.

Next, the team defined an ideal state, based on the core mission. Being in the "glup" business, the team members said they wanted most to maximize return on investment and to create a work environment that would ensure effective work and growth of the staff. Examining the current practice of assigning five people to a shift, for example, the team discovered that having six people instead might make more economic and social sense. Rather than simply having the minimum number of workers needed, there would be extra resources readily available so that replacements could be drawn whenever there were an illness, tardiness, or other difficulty.

The design team, after examining the way supplies came into the line, devised a method of materials flow control based on cutting out unnecessary bureaucratic channels. The person in the position on the production line where the raw materials were received would not only be responsible for making sure there was inventory, but would have a direct line to the warehouse as well. This change eliminated the necessity of going through three levels of management.

The team also looked at the technology of breakdowns and found that it would be possible for the various lines to have fewer technicians. Line operators would learn some first-level maintenance, previously done by technicians, while the reduced number of specialists could form a pool available to handle problems that cropped up anywhere.

Everyone was put on an annual wage, based on both job function and personal expertise. From the outset, all workers were treated as multitask workers, capable of covering several positions. Everyone started as a technician IV, able to do three of the five jobs on a shift; as people learned other jobs, they were upgraded to technician III, II, and ultimately the top grade. Decisions as to who would cover which position on what shift were left to be dealt with by the team.

In recruiting work staff for the new plant, the company went to the community, which had a large population of unemployed blacks. The company officials talked with community leaders and offered employment to the local residents. The leaders indicated that the community would prefer to have as many people working as possible, even if not full time. As a result, the company decided to hire larger numbers of people working shorter weeks.

The original design committee was eventually replaced by a plant manager's work team, which included people at all levels in the plant. The design of every aspect of each task, including the work environment, was to be planned, implemented, and reviewed by those who would be performing those tasks. This approach has been successful; for several years the plant's productivity has been about 20 percent higher than that of other plants in the system making the same product.

Case 2: A Midstate Medical Center. A large medical school was faced with some crucial choices about the priorities of its activities and the allocation of its financial and human resources. The school was located in a village several hundred miles from the main university's hospital facilities. A small community hospital served as a training location for some of the medical students; many others had to do their field practice in larger hospitals elsewhere in the state.

Many of the school's faculty members were highly competent both in the basic sciences and in clinical practices such as medicine and surgery. In times past, research grants had provided much of the funding for the basic sciences; but such grants were no longer easily obtainable. Because the small community was unable to provide much income through patient care, the school would now need to raise money by increasing the number of hospital beds and, even more important, expanding the level of outpatient care. But such a program would divert money and faculty resources from research.

The dean faced a serious dilemma in defining the medical school's direction. Many of the faculty members, obviously, wanted to maintain the emphasis on research; the hospital administration wanted to increase the cost-effectiveness of patient care; and the local citizens, along with significant members of the board of trustees, wanted an increase in service to the community.

The dean called a conference of key representatives of the major constituencies: the hospital director, top faculty members, university administrators, and the like. Using an open-systems planning model, they set about their first and most important task — identifying the core mission of the school. After a great deal of discussion, debate, and conflict, they concluded, not too enthusiastically, that the core mission of this particular school must be the training of doctors for delivering care to the community. This decision would mean some changes in budget allocations, some probable loss of present faculty, and probable difficulties in recruiting distinguished new faculty.

Having determined the core mission, the conference members could then study the domains making demands on the school administration, review the present responses, and develop a strategy for different responses based on a clarified awareness of the core mission. In the process of working through the model, they found that they would be better able to maintain faculty excellence and research capability than they had feared.

The committee carried out the major reorientation of the

medical center toward the improvement of delivery and training of doctors for primary, or direct, care. This effort has changed the recruitment of faculty from research oriented to delivery oriented candidates. Today the quality of the school's faculty and research is average or above. The training and education the medical students receive are considered first class, and the school has significantly expanded its community service, even though it has lost some faculty and a number of activities have had to be redesigned.

Case 3: A Western School of Medicine. A large, distinguished western medical school used the same process as in Case 2, but arrived at the opposite conclusion. This school decided that its core mission was to maintain the quality of its biomedical research. The school wished to train doctors primarily for graduate activities on the cutting edge of applied science; it was less concerned about training the general practitioner, and only minimally interested in providing health care to the local community, in part because there was already a quite adequate distribution of physicians in the area surrounding the school.

Summary

Where there is complexity in an organization, there is likely to be a conflict of priorities not only about goals, but also about the nature of the organization's reason for existing. In view of the social, ecological, and economic interdependency in today's environment, management will likely want to clarify the priorities of the organization's current mission. If the mission is first separated from the goals and independently defined, goals and priorities can be set within a context of agreement about the nature of the organization.

Once the core mission is agreed upon, it is often desirable to start the planning process by looking at the demands of the environment on the enterprise, rather than the other way around. Once these demands have been identified and a "snapshot" of the current response system recorded, change managers can be much more confident, and probably more accurate as well, in developing strategic plans for moving the organization ahead. They can also be more aware of the likelihood of resistance to change in turbulent times and can plan strategies for coping with it.

In all three cases presented, the clear definition of the core mission provided guidelines for setting priorities, establishing management and recruitment systems, and other necessary activities within the institution. The methodology of open-systems planning can, we feel, be useful for working through the complex issues facing current organizations.

3

Dynamics of Organizations

Where Change Occurs

Like the six blind men who gave widely varying descriptions of an elephant according to what portion of the animal lay under their grasp, so can we look at an organization from a number of different perspectives. We offer here three ways of describing organizations. The last of the three, "the input–output system," will be a guiding principle as we move on to discuss the change process itself in Chapter 4.

Organizations as Social Systems

A social system is one in which the subsystems each have their own identities and purposes, but their activities must be coordinated or the parent system cannot function. For example, the human body contains a nervous system, a muscular system, and a circulatory system, all of which must be integrated to maintain life. In the same way, an organization has production, sales, finance, and development activities, which must all be integrated.

Organizations as Political Systems

In the classic political power system, people at the top have more power in most matters than people at the bottom. Political behavior (sometimes called "strategy") is behavior designed to further the goals of a person or group, more or less regardless of the effect on others. It is "getting the votes." Some rules of political-system behavior are vastly different from rules of social-system behavior (see Fig. 3–1). Some managers in organizations operate under social-system rules, others under political-system rules. No wonder there are "communication problems"!

Organizations as Input–Output Systems

Organizations can also be viewed as *input–output systems*, transforming *needs* and *raw materials* into *services* and *products* (see Fig. 3–2).

In addition, one must consider the attitudes, values, be-

	Social System	**Political System**
Feedback to Subordinates	*Always* provide open feedback on positive and negative aspects of behavior. Emphasize the positive; support and reinforce.	*Never* trust positive feedback from immediate boss; there will always be a "price tag" included. Trust third-party feedback but not from direct supervisor.
Decision Making	Get facts quickly; make decisions; take risks.	Never make decisions until the *last* possible moment. Keep your options open.

Figure 3–1
System Norms

Input	**Transformed by Organization**	**Output**
Needs + Raw materials	⟶	Services + Products
Example		
Information + Computer technology	⟶	Information systems / Computers, software

Figure 3–2
Input-Output Systems

liefs, and priorities of the organization leaders. For example, if *quality* is all-important as a priority, structures and tasks must be organized to achieve optimum quality in the process of moving inputs to outputs. Careful inspection of raw material, decisions close to the work flow, distributed power — all support such a priority.

Since the quality, aesthetics, and price of the output (product or service), as defined by customers, determine market share, it is crucial that managers of improvement, innovation, and quality use the principles of managing change.

Effectiveness in Organizations

In today's complex world, organization leaders *determine* the culture. The managerial strategy and the rewards in the organization. The environment, including new technologies, telecommunications, and better information systems, has an impact on the effectiveness of the managerial strategy.

Characteristics of Effective Organizations

We have found that *effective* organizations tend to have common and predictable characteristics. We developed this list a decade ago, but we are convinced of its relevance today.

1. An effective organization tends to be *purposeful* and *goal oriented.* The leadership, heads of functions and programs, and individual units and people have, in addition to day-to-day goals, some relatively explicit long-term objectives.
2. *Form follows function.* The way work is organized, resources allocated, and decisions are made is defined by the *work* requirements, not by authority or power requirements. Power is widely dispersed and differentiated from (official) authority on the organization chart.
3. Decisions are made based on sources of information rather than position in the hierarchy.
4. Reward systems are related to the task rather than the status of the performer. Attention is paid to intrinsic as well as extrinsic rewards; for example, the lower paid pediatrician's work is no less *valued* than the higher paid surgeon's work.
5. Communication is relatively open. The norms or ground rules of this system reward the expression of differences of opinion on ideas, solutions to problems, goals, and so on, regardless of the authority relationship of the parties in disagreement.
6. Inappropriate competition is minimized; collaboration is rewarded where it is in the organization's best interests.
7. Conflict is managed, not suppressed or avoided. The management of conflicts over ideas, work, and other issues is seen as an essential part of everyone's job.
8. The organization is viewed as an open system, embedded in a complex environment whose components are constantly making demands. The management of this group of demands is a major task of the executive.
9. Management makes a conscious effort to support each individual's identity, integrity, and freedom. Work and rewards are organized to maintain these values.
10. The organization operates in a *learning* mode. It sees itself as always "in process," continually assessing the current state of things and consciously planning im-

provements. There are built-in feedback mechanisms ("How are we doing?") at all levels.

To review, we have proposed several ways to view an organization: as a social system, a political system, or an input–output system. The latter perspective guides our following examination of the change process. We believe the *work* of the organization is the key factor that must be changed if output (products and services) are to be improved or optimized.

We have briefly observed some of the characteristics of organizations that focus on work. We now proceed to the change process itself.

4

The Change Process

Why Change?

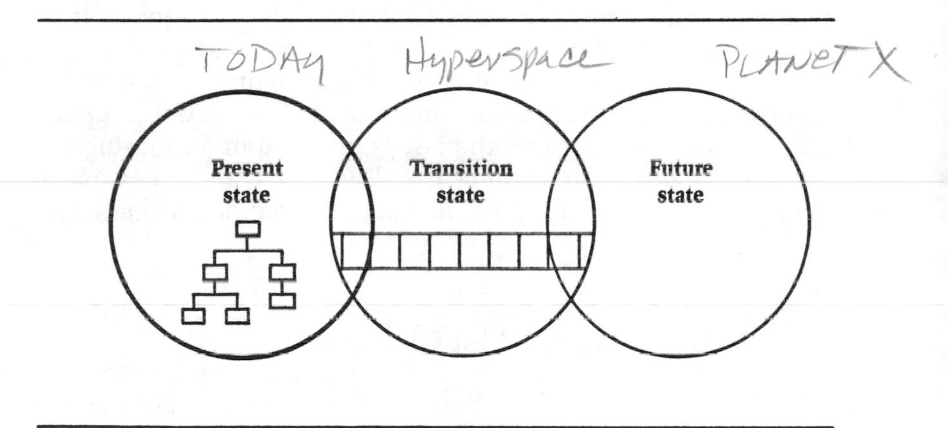

It may be stating the obvious to say that any major organizational change involves three distinct conditions: the *future state,* where the leadership wants the organization to get to; the *present state,* where the organization currently is; and the *transition state,* the set of conditions and activities that the organization must go through to move from the present to the future.

Thinking about the change process as involving these three states helps clarify the work to be done in managing major change — *defining* the future state, *assessing* the present, and *managing* the transition.

The change process in a large complex system has several aspects:

- Setting goals and defining the *future state,* or organizational conditions desired after the change.
- Diagnosing the *present condition* in relation to those goals.
- Defining the *transition state:* activities and commitments required to reach the future state.
- Developing strategies and action plans for managing this transition.

Change management is not a neat, sequential process. The initial tasks of defining the future state and assessing present conditions demand simultaneous attention. Figure 4–1 illustrates the reciprocity of these early steps. Understandably, the question is: Where does one start?

Organizational change must start by defining the need for change, for it is this question that provides the initial impetus. This chapter will focus on the issues involved in diagnosing the need for change, determining the degree of choice that exists about whether to change, and identifying what needs changing.

Defining the Need for Change

The forces requiring change in large systems today tend to originate *outside* the organization. Changes in legislation, market demand resulting from worldwide competition, availability of resources, development of new technology, and social priorities frequently necessitate that organization managers redesign the organizational structures and procedures, redefine their priorities, and redeploy their resources. Two sample areas are discussed below.

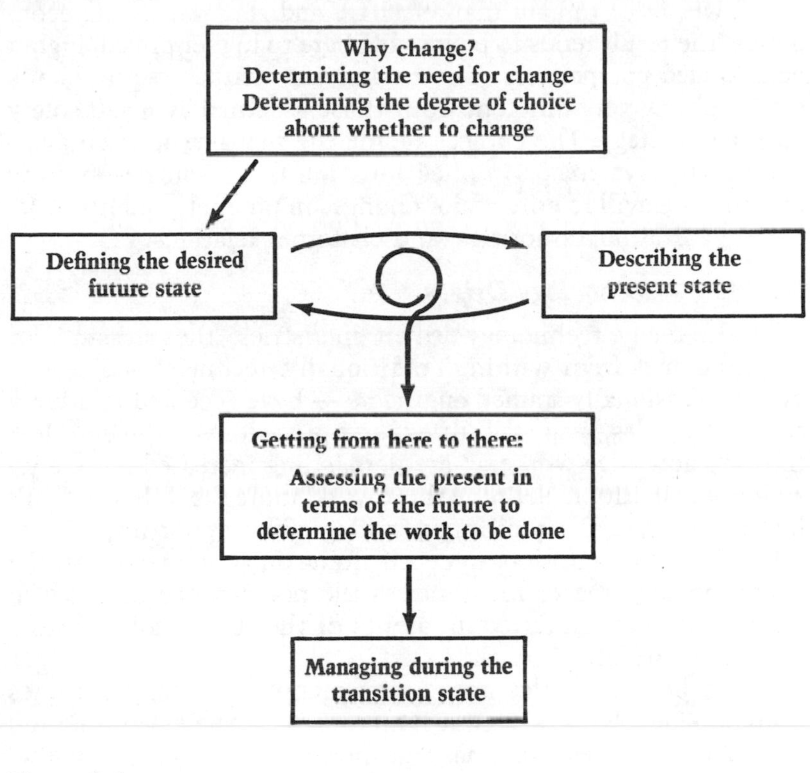

Figure 4–1
Map of the Change Management Process

Changes in Socioeconomics

One source of pressure for change derives from shifts in the socioeconomic makeup of the population. In both developed and developing nations, increased affluence within the population has resulted in greater demand for higher value-added products and services. In the United States the trend, some would argue, has reached the point where quality and service have replaced price as the prime criteria in the decision to buy. For businesses that have long held that the way to enhance revenue is to sell more at a lower price to gain market share and thus gain scale economies, the result tends to be loss of share to higher-priced, higher value-added competitors. The underlying market requirements are becoming very different from those assumed by a sell solely on price strategy. The choices facing the manager in such a situation all have major implications for the organization. Any choice made will require major changes in products, quality, pricing, organizational priorities, and customer relations.

New Technology Drives

In many technology-driven industries, the pressure for change comes from within. Traditionally, technical workers — even professionally trained engineers — have accepted relatively structured roles, responsibilities, and procedures as given. Now those "knowledge workers" are demanding increased autonomy and responsibility in defining their work, more flexibility in work hours, rules, and procedures, and greater opportunities for achievement recognition. In determining an action response, the institutional manager must assess the potency of this force in light of the economic requirements of the institution, and the customers' needs.

In both examples above, the pressure for change comes from outside the management structure; nevertheless, any action taken, or lack of response, has significant consequences.

Stating the Change Problem

The need for change is frequently described in terms of "symptoms." One important dividend of a good organizational diagnosis is an accurate statement of the problem that necessitates a change. Consider a situation in which the problem is defined as "poor morale" in a department or throughout the organization, or "poor coordination" between the sales and manufacturing divisions. It would seem to follow that the change strategy should try to improve morale through some satisfaction-improvement activities or a communications-improvement program. Such direct strategies can work if the symptom statement describes the *fundamental* condition needing change.

A more likely-to-succeed strategy, however, would follow the diagnosis of those symptoms with the question *why* — what might be causing the problems of morale or lack of coordination. For example, a school superintendent in a large school system stated that there was a morale problem among the teachers in the district and that something must be done to improve morale. Implicit in this declaration of need was a goal statement that if morale improved, something would be significantly better in the system. The appropriate diagnostic questions in this instance are: "What would be different or better?" and "How much does it matter?"

If the answer to the first question were that higher teacher morale would improve students' reading levels, the superintendent would face one set of choices. If the answer were that teachers would not call in sick so often if morale were improved, that would be another issue. If an improvement in students' reading levels were the school's main objective, the diagnosis would probably focus on poor teacher morale as a "cause" of the low reading levels. If a lower absentee rate for teachers were the goal rationale, the focus would be on understanding why teachers are using their sick leave. In each instance, what needs changing is not simply the teachers' morale, but some other more primary organizational condition.

The Degree of Choice About Whether to Change

An apparently obvious, but very often overlooked, question is whether the organizational leadership can decide *whether* to make a change, or only *how* to make it. Before deciding on a change strategy, the executive must determine how much control or influence he or she has over the conditions providing the stimulus for changing in the first place.

Sometimes external demands or forces provide the necessity for a change. In that case, the members of the leadership have no choice but to cope with the demand for change. Examples are legislation concerning environmental pollution, minority hiring, or the allocation of public funds to health care services; new laws providing for educational parity for handicapped children; import regulations limiting product sales in a particular area; and successful union demands for increased benefits or power.

In other situations, the need for change is stimulated by forces either within or outside the organization, but nonetheless under management's general control. These include such conditions as the need for reorganization because of a reorientation from a technology-driven organization to a market-driven one; the need to add new functions and departments to a medical school due to breakthroughs in medical knowledge; the demand for increasing worker control over production; the need for increased product quality for customer satisfaction; and the need to increase control or efficiency through the introduction of new technology or office automation. In these types of situations, the manager can choose not only *how* to manage the change, but also *whether* to initiate it at all.

It might be useful to arrange the elements on a grid (see Fig. 4–2). On one axis we can list the *sources* of the factors concerned with change, such as owners/directors, legislators, employees, trade unions, special-interest and pressure groups, customers, and social values. On the other axis we can identify the *potency* of the force — high, medium, or low. Management can then array the forces operating in the situation according to both constituency and urgency. Additionally, the position of the various forces for or against the change can be designated with plus or minus signs. Such a display provides some perspective about what has to be taken into account before forming any specific action strategy.

A couple of issues are critical in conducting such an analysis. First, the management must make sure that its information about the situation is accurate and complete. The nature of the change in question should be clearly understood, and the position of each "source" regarding that change should be accurately assessed. Second, the manager's own biases and blind spots must be recognized and overcome in order for the analysis to be useful. There is often a tendency to "misperceive" or generalize about the potency of particular sources, following the assumption that these sources have always been "strong" or "weak" and that their potency in the current situation will be comparable to that in

Nature of change demanded: ____________

Potency of Forces	Owners	Legislature	Employees	Trade Unions	Social Values
High					
Medium					
Low					

Figure 4–2
Sample Grid for Analyzing the Sources and Potency of Forces for Change

previous issues. To combat this tendency, it is often helpful to consider the future potency of each force *presuming that the management response to the demanded changes remains largely the same as at present.*

Case Illustration 1: External Forces for Change — No Choice About Making the Change

The national manager of a multinational organization was faced with a dilemma. Concerned over environmental pollution, the mayors of two major cities in his host country had issued proclamations prohibiting the purchase of the type of product sold by his company and his competitors. If these proclamations became effective, the organization's business would cease completely.

In analyzing the dilemma, the manager studied several long-standing conditions. For one, his firm had a strong policy of not colluding with competitors. In addition, current company policies restricted the manager's methods of interacting with the communities in which he did business. If he obeyed the policies to the letter, he would have no alternative but to shut down his business.

To break the deadlock between company policy and local conditions, the manager had to help the firm's owners recognize the differences between the culture in which he was operating and that of the parent company. Finally, he was allowed to do some "experimenting" with relationships with competitors in the host country. Under the new strategy, he met with his counterparts in competing organizations. Together they were able to find a constitutional lawyer, who discovered some laws on the books of the host country limiting the power of mayors to make proclamations in restraint of trade. Based on this information, the managers were able to get a restraining order, which gave them time to attend to the substantive question of whether their products were in fact harmful to the environment. The manager saw that of the two competing forces acting on him — internal company policy and external local demands — he had to respond primarily to the host country forces in order to deal with the basic issue of product marketability.

In addition to a complex managerial choice of which way to move and with what consequences, the manager needed to recognize that he had no choice about whether to respond to the pressure from the host country. In most of his previous managerial actions, his orientation had been to the company — the owners. From that perspective, he had made choices about how to cope with the host country in a wide variety of situations. By analyzing the types of forces now operating and becoming aware of his lack of choice about whether to change, the manager was able to put his energy into creative strategies for how to effect the necessary change.

Case Illustration 2: Conflicting Perceptions of the Necessity for Change

The management committee and chief executive of a large manufacturing company were confronted with an increasingly serious morale problem among middle management, including the threat of unionization of the professional and technical staff. The company was a large, decentralized organization with a number of profit centers, or business divisions, and a strong headquarters organization. In the past few years, the increasing influence of the trade unions, as well as progressive practices by the management, had resulted in changes such as new, creative work designs, improved quality of working life on the shop floor, and better compensation plans. A great deal of energy had been put into improving relationships and redistributing earnings between owners and workers, particularly those represented by the trade unions. Relatively little attention had been paid to salaried nonunion staff. These employees had been most hurt by inflation and other economic problems; their morale was at an all-time low. Many professional and technical people, as well as junior management staff, felt that their only option was to organize and join trade unions.

Attempts to communicate this state of affairs to the organization's leadership had been stifled, either at the division management level or through central management's not "hearing" the messages. Personnel staff and others in the organization had sent several messages to the management group and to the chief executive, reporting the problem and outlining its potential implications. For a variety of reasons, the chief executive and several members of the management committee chose to treat the entire condition as a minor upset that could be smoothed over.

The chief executive had personally visited several field operations, and what he saw was, naturally, quite inconsistent with the written reports from his staff. For him, the "objective" evidence of loyal and happy people who produced, and thereby increased profitability and productivity, was clear and overriding; he was unable to see that there was real trouble afoot. As he was approaching retirement, he did not want to initiate any major program that would upset the good performance results that had been achieved, even if a morale problem did exist, which he doubted.

The retirement of the chief executive preceded by six months the assumption of office by his successor. At the time of the announcement of the new appointment, the new chief executive, who had been on the management committee, shared the retiring chief executive's attitudes toward the morale condition; neither one saw it as a major priority for top-management effort. However, the new designate wanted to get a personal look at the general state of affairs and attitudes in the organization before he officially took office.

Aided by staff and consultants, the new chief executive arranged a series of "listening meetings," in which he would visit each field operation and listen to the concerns of groups of staff members. The membership of the groups was developed by a formula involving lateral representation in several areas as well as personnel from different hierarchical levels, meeting in a "diagonal slice" group. In addition to division managers, the status levels included middle managers, professional and technical staff, administrative and support people, shop stewards, shop workers, and new employees, so that the "diagonal slice" group was fully representative of the total field organization. During these visits, the new chief executive became acutely aware of, and deeply concerned about, the true state of affairs.

After completing his visits, he convened his top-management group and announced to his colleagues that he planned to spend up to 20 percent of his working time on the issue of employee morale. He personally took on the role of project manager, instituting a series of monthly meetings with operating managers at various levels so as to monitor continually the state of affairs. He urged heads of functions and businesses to conduct such activities as well. A senior field manager was assigned to study and recommend changes in both compensation and reward allocation to lower- and middle-management groups. He built in a feedback system through the line organization, which required his immediate subordinates to have up-to-date information on the attitudes of middle and junior management. The results included a significant improvement in morale; some changes in decision making authority; a number of improvements in getting products to the market faster; and some significant cost savings.

In this illustration, we can compare strategies of managing the situation by two chief executives who made opposing diagnoses of the same set of forces. With the incumbent executive, the impulses for change within the organization were relayed indirectly, through memos and reports from the staff to the organization management. This information from the staff was not validated by his own experience in his routine visits to the field; therefore, his diagnosis of the strength and importance of the forces for change from the field was almost totally erroneous. By contrast, the desire of the second chief executive to find out the real situation for himself enabled him to assess more accurately the strength of the forces. From his own field testing, he recognized that he did not have a real choice about whether to respond to these forces. His actions, his personal commitment of time and energy, and his follow-up in maintaining a flow of information throughout the system resulted from a different diagnosis of the same set of conditions. His strategy for managing the situation was very different from that of his predecessor.

Case Illustration 3: Management Control Over Whether to Change — Misperception of Potency of Internal Forces

Case 2 above involved forces both internal and external to the organization. The first chief executive responded primarily (albeit inaccurately) to the internal forces; he did not recognize the potency of the environment — economic conditions — on the people in the organization. In the following case the reverse is true; the external force is very well understood. The chief executive recognizes its clear potency and chooses to respond to it actively, but is unaware of the potency of the internal forces resistant to carrying out those actions.

Background and Initial Strategy. The company had long been recognized as the leading maker, in innovation and quality, of a sophisticated electronics product. The firm was organized into several decentralized divisions, each serving a different industry. The company's image of product quality and reliability had long enabled each division to maintain higher prices and profit margins than competitors. Recently, however, due to increased price and quality competition, the firm's share of market began to drop. The chief executive decided that in order to protect its profit margins and market share, his organization should take a strongly customer-centered posture and focus attention on developing a strong value-added product and customer service component. He wanted the organization managers at all levels to be actively concerned with increasing customer service and customer satisfaction. He made his position very clear to his top-management group (division general managers and corporate staff vice-presidents), and personally visited the field to talk with plant managers, sales managers, and engineering design managers. He wrote and distributed several memos and papers that defined his philosophy about this new image for the company, and offered corporate staff resources to assist the divisions in carrying out an active program.

Diagnosis. After a year of operating under this change strategy, it became very clear to the chief executive that it was not working. Diagnosis revealed that although the chief executive officer had the *official* authority and power as the leader of the organization, the *actual* power to change behavior was more widely distributed. The CEO did not "own" anyone who invented, manufactured, sold, or serviced a product, nor did he "own" any customers. *His* attitudes and values were seen by middle managers as much less relevant than those of the division senior managers. The middle managers were responding according to their perception of what behavior was rewarded or punished in the organization; the CEO's exhortations and personal biases did not affect them, particularly since many of his immediate subordinates did not echo his position. On the contrary, the general managers were all from engineering or manufacturing backgrounds and believed that quality and technological innovation should be their sole considerations. In their view, engineering should design the product right, manufacturing should efficiently provide high-quality products, and sales should sell the quality and sophistication of the product. Value-added features such as increased service and attention to customer convenience were viewed as nice but expendable amenities; given declining revenues, the general managers felt they could not afford to increase the service organization or pay much attention to customer convenience. On reflection, the CEO realized that he had contributed to this perception. During top-management meetings, the bulk of the time was always spent focusing on cost control and on pushing sales volume; little time was ever left to discuss the customer-service agenda. The result was that the division general managers and their subordinate managers felt safe in following a "minimum compliance" strategy: do the minimum to appease the chief executive.

Revised Strategy and Action Steps. On recognizing the situation, the CEO set about directly to change the organization's behavior. At that time, one of the division general manager positions fell vacant, and the CEO decided to assume his duties himself while he sought a replacement. This gave him the opportunity to role model what he expected from his other general managers and to learn firsthand what worked and what didn't. Within the division he was running, he met with all managers and again outlined his agenda. They identified goals, actions, and timetables for getting started on this new thrust. In his CEO role, he made it a norm to start every meeting with a report from each executive on what his or her division had achieved in the area of customer service enhancement — and he always reported first on his own division. He placed responsibility on all staff vice-presidents to treat the operating divisions as "customers" and to report on what they were doing to provide value-added service to the divisions.

He used the company's annual senior management conference, attended by the top sixty people in the firm, as a companywide sharing of experiences, lessons learned, and plans on the topic of "customer caring." He announced at this three-day event that customer caring would be the theme for senior management conferences not just this year, but for the foreseeable future.

In preparation for the conference, each division conducted a telephone survey of its customers on their perceptions of the company's products, service, and degree of caring about the customer's needs. The results were tabulated, and at the first session of the conference, each general manager was assigned to report the *companywide* findings on certain aspects of the survey. Division groups defined visions and goals consistent with becoming a "customer-driven" organization. Next, functional groupings (across divisions) discussed how they could support those visions. Each division then devised strategies and actions for the next six months for achieving the stated goals. Finally, each of the sixty division managers present stated, one by one in front of the entire group, what personal actions he or she promised to take in the following thirty days in support of the division's plan.

The CEO required each manager to submit his or her action commitments in writing within three days, and asked for a one-page report in six weeks describing what had been done and what was planned for the next two-month period. He also announced that the entire group would reconvene in five or six months to share their experiences and plan the next steps. Three days later, one hour before close of business, the chief executive called the four managers whose written action promises he had not received, and told them to have their reports on his desk within twelve hours. News of this action traveled throughout the organization, including overseas locations, within twenty-four hours.

The message was received loud and clear. Over the next several months, behaviors changed dramatically: engineers were out visiting customers, manufacturing people were meeting with customer service staff, sales representatives were visiting plants, and executives were regularly calling customers.

Here the executive manager did not initially recognize that his control over whether or not to make the change he desired was constrained by the behavior and attitudes of people in the organization.

Summary

We have argued that the first order of concern in developing a change strategy must be determination of the *need for*

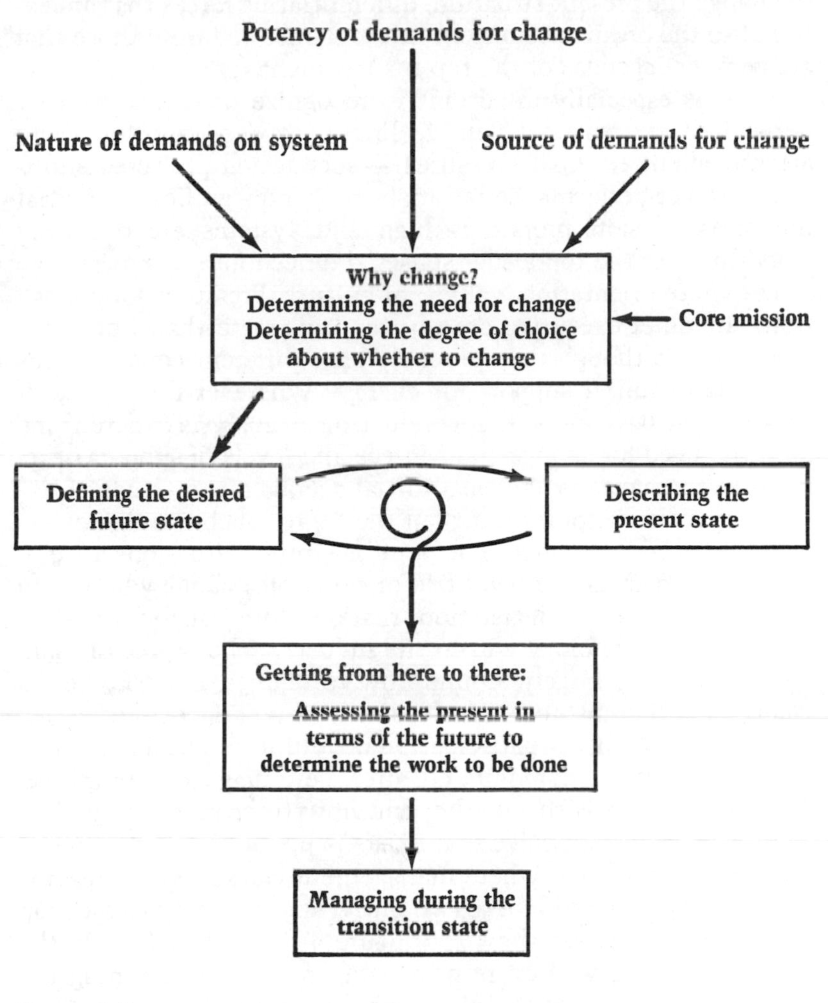

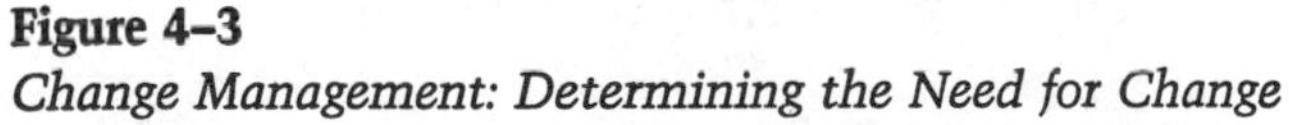

Figure 4–3
Change Management: Determining the Need for Change

change. This means locating and assessing the sources of pressure to change the present situation; differentiating forces that are external to the organization from internal ones and from those that are personal agendas of the top management.

It is especially important to recognize the pressures that derive from the personal "gut" feelings of top leaders. Often there are no salient external pressures — recent and projected short-term market performance is satisfactory; no significant internal pressures — staff morale is high and systems are operating smoothly; yet the top leader senses the need for a major change in corporate orientation, values, or culture. Pressures for change from the chief executive are no less legitimate than from anywhere else, although they probably have different consequences in terms of initial support for change. Whatever the source of pressure, we have found that conducting an analysis to determine both the need for change and sources and levels of support or resistance to change is a critical initial agenda for top leadership.

It is also helpful to sort out the degree of choice that exists about *whether to change.* The point is simple: situations arise in which an organization has little or no choice about whether to change, such as new legislation, market shifts, or the introduction of new technology within the industry. The degree of managerial choice is largely around *how to change,* not whether to change. In other instances, such as new market opportunities, acquisition possibilities, participation in voluntary social programs, and even changing corporate culture, there may exist a managerial choice about both *whether* and *how* to change. Being clear about the degree of choice that exists is helpful in that it directs attention to the areas where management can have an impact.

We can now add these two initial analysis tasks to the map of the change process shown in Figure 4–1 (see Fig. 4–3). In the next chapter we will examine what's involved in defining the "place we want to get to," the desired future state.

5

Defining the Future State

The great management theorist Casey Stengel, former manager of the New York Yankees, once said: "If you don't know where you're going, you might end up somewhere else." Any change has some *end state,* a condition or set of conditions that defines completion of the particular change, or at least a point of measurement.

Visions—Missions—End States—Midpoint Goals

Today more and more attention is being paid, in both the planning process and determination of managerial strategies, to articulating the "vision," or desired end state, of the leaders and managers of the change. Although it is extremely important, and certainly motivating and exciting (at least for the top leaders), defining the vision alone is not enough to produce the kind of organizational energy that will achieve a change. Likewise, we observe a great deal of attention devoted to clarifying the organization's core mission as a prelude to planned change. Again, though it is extremely important for the leadership to be clear about the definition of its core mission, clarity of mission alone does not mobilize sufficient energy to make the change happen. In addition to articulating the vision, which is usually abstract, and clarifying the mission, which is often quite general, it is necessary to specify a *midpoint goal.* The midpoint goal, or "future state" description, represents a desirable organizational condition intermediate between the present state and the achievement of the vision. Frequently the vision is a context toward which the achievement of the midpoint goal is a key step. For example, if the organization wants a new approach to distribution in effect within eighteen months, where does it want to be in six months? What should that midpoint look like? One must have clear and detailed midpoint goals in order to motivate the members of an organization to make a real commitment of time, energy, and resources.

Determining the Future State: An Early Agenda

We have found that the greatest single threat to successful change results from inadequate *early* attention to defining the desired *end states* for the change, both the ultimate vision and the interim future state (midpoint goal). As we said earlier, organizational change must by definition start from where we are — the present. However, there is a significant danger that thinking and action may become trapped by the present, particularly by the problems identified in the present, so that creativity in goal setting and problem solving may be stifled by fears of impracticability. Managers can help free up their thinking by momentarily ignoring the present and concentrating on the future.

Once the need for change and the degree of choice about changing have been determined, the next step in the change process is for the organization's management to develop a detailed description of the desired midpoint condition. This description of the interim future state for the organization should specify the expected organizational structure, reward system, personnel policies, authority and task-responsibility distributions, managerial values and practices, performance-review systems, relationships with external groups, and expected organizational performance outcomes. We advise that the description of the desired future, especially where organizational structure and processes are concerned, be guided by a framework of ideas about effective organizations, either developed by the top manager or gleaned from management writings. For example, the list of "Characteristics of Effective Organizations" discussed in Chapter 3 (see pages 27–28) offers such a framework. Likewise, the attributes of superior-performing or "excellent" companies described in books such as *In Search of Excellence* and *A Passion for Excellence* also may provide useful perspectives.[1]

The "future state" should describe the change leadership's view of the organization at a *specific time* far enough in the future to provide a sense of the feasibility of the projected changes. State the *specific date,* for example, 1 January 1990, for the achievement of the future state. Finally, the future state description should be developed bearing in mind the *core mission* of the enterprise.

Writing a Midpoint Scenario

We have found that it frequently helps managers to refine their description of the future state by writing a scenario of what the organization should look like at the intermediate (e.g., midpoint). Scenario writing involves first selecting a specific time for the midpoint. For example, if the end state is a merger of two major functions into one new operating unit, to be achieved in one year — where do you want to be five months from now (or at some other significant intermediate point)? In scenario preparation, the task is to write a *detailed, behaviorally oriented scenario* that describes what one would expect to see, hear, even feel, in the projected situation at the specified point in time. Imagine yourself in a helicopter, photographing several days' worth of activity with a camera that has a very wide angle lens. Spell out in writing the detail that the camera would see. In the merger ex-

[1]Thomas J. Peters and Robert H. Waterman, Jr., *In Search of Excellence: Lessons From America's Best-Run Companies* (New York: Harper & Row, 1982); Thomas J. Peters and Nancy Austin, *A Passion for Excellence: The Leadership Difference* (New York: Random House, 1985).

ample given above, where would the functions be at the five-month point? Which subunits would be operating in the old mode, which in the new mode, and which in a temporary state that is neither? Who would be managing which parts of the work? What would be the information flow? Who would be responsible for what decisions, and why? What would be the attitude of the staff in these subunits toward the change?

This advice about developing a future state description and intermediate scenario should not be viewed as an invitation to fantasize away your problems. It offers, rather, a method for codifying, in as firm a way as possible, the world you really desire to live in. This certainly should be consistent with the core mission of the enterprise, and equally important, be *realistic* and *attainable.* It represents a personalized description of what you, as the change manager, are committed to achieving. As such, the tasks of developing the future state description and midpoint scenario cannot be delegated; they cannot be exclusively a staff product. While staff can make input into their development, both must be thoroughly planned out by the organizational leadership.

Advantages of Defining the Future State

Several benefits derive from the obviously significant effort involved in developing a detailed description of the future state. First, and most obvious, is that the effort results in a clear and detailed "blueprint" of the future organization, which can guide the development of a change strategy. We noted earlier that the single greatest threat to successful change is the lack of early attention to defining the end state. The timely establishment of clear and detailed goals for the change effort yields the following dividends:

- Optimism replaces pessimism as the driving force in considering the possibilities for managing the change
- The detailed behavior spelled out in the description of the future allows members of the organization to visualize their own role in the change, improving employee compliance

- The description of the future state specifies the nature of the projected changes and offers a rationale for managerial actions, reducing uncertainty
- The task pulls management away from the tendency to attack symptoms and "solve problems" and focuses attention on defining what's needed to make the organization effective

Let's briefly discuss each of these elements.

Optimism

When defining our visions and objectives, we tend to be positive about future possibilities, describing a situation that we would find favorable and desirable to experience. For executives involved in defining a future state, the process provides a motivating and positive tension to get on with the work of achieving that future. By contrast, an initial focus on the necessarily imperfect present state tends to magnify negative experiences and the possibility of failure, inviting a pessimistic orientation. Fears of faultfinding and rationalization often distract the planners from getting on with the work of changing the situation.

Case Illustration

The chief executive and the chief operating officers of a relatively small ($50 million in sales) engineering and manufacturing firm decided to establish a five-year goal of expanding the company to $150 million in sales. The company had grown very slowly over several decades, and the new goal of tripling sales volume in five years implied a dramatic departure from previous methods of operating. A task force composed of the heads of all functions was made responsible for developing a plan for achieving the corporate goal. The organization's top functional leadership publicly expressed enthusiasm and commitment to the growth goals. However, privately they thought the organization incapable of achieving such a goal. They felt that they lacked the marketing competence and the manufacturing and field service capacity to support the projected volume of work. For six months following the announcement of the goal, the task force did little except meet regularly and produce internal reports, which identified a multitude of problems and drew conclusions that the goal was unrealistic.

In frustration, the CEO and chief operating officer scheduled a three-day retreat with all heads of function and their immediate subordinate managers. The agenda for the retreat was to develop a comprehensive vision of what the organization would be like when the goal was achieved five years hence. Each participant was asked to think about what the organization would be doing, particularly in his or her functional area, *"five years from now when we are a $150 million operation."* They were told not to be constrained in their thinking with concerns about "how do we get there."

The retreat, attended by the organization's top twenty-five managers and actively led by the CEO, began with a review of the products currently being sold, their pricing structure, and the nature and needs of the consumer market they were trying to reach. This focus on the market led to identifying new "products," some of which were actually services, in contrast to the company's traditional "hardware-type" products. New "customers" were targeted in industries and functions outside of those traditionally served; new distribution routes and methods that enhanced their dealer relationships were discovered. Perhaps the most significant outcome of the exercise was the identification of new sources of revenue from "service products," which did not require the kind of major front-end capitalization associated with enormous manufacturing expansion. Enthusiasm grew among the management participants as all functions took part in developing the future scenario.

On the second day, each of the functional management groups met separately to define what its area would look like in terms of structure, personnel skills and numbers, facilities, decision responsibilities, and the nature of its work. On the third day, each function presented its "scenario" for open discussion. The retreat ended with each group's being assigned to devise a plan for achieving the agreed upon "future state" for its area. A one-day meeting was scheduled for thirty days later to report and discuss the plans.

During those thirty days, lots of cross-functional meetings were held to coordinate the planning. The plans presented at the follow-up meeting were fairly detailed and realistic. The same group of organization leaders who for six months had held that "it" (the achievement of the ambiguous end state) wasn't feasible, when pushed to define "it," developed the future state scenario and plans for achieving it in one month. The difference was in large part the result of being forced to let go temporarily of the present and the responsibility for figuring out *how* to achieve the ambiguous and threatening goal, and shifting attention to the future and the encouraging task of defining *what should be* achieved.

Identifying with the End State

The detail provided by a comprehensive description of the future provides the necessary information for those not involved in the definition process to understand what is desired. More important, it improves their ability to determine how they might fit into the future. *Misperception* of the implications of a change for one's own future role and responsibilities is a major cause of resistance to change. Resistance can be significantly overcome by providing employees with sufficient information about the end state to provide a more accurate perception about their future role in the organization — and to reassure them that they will indeed have a role to play.

Overcoming Resistance to Change. In the illustration above there was much initial confusion and uncertainty among the company's managers as to how and whether they would fit into a rapidly growing organization. Due to the past slow growth, employment was stable; most employees had been with the company for their entire career. Several of the managers, and even a few functional heads, had worked their way up in the company over a number of years. While feeling competent with their current responsibilities, many were unsure of how they would operate or manage in a different context. The announcement of the growth goal without a detailed description of how the organization would run led to widespread misperceptions. Employees in manufacturing envisioned major upsets in the manufacturing technology and processes; marketing and sales personnel saw a dramatic shift away from their personal relationships with and support of dealer networks; engineering and research and development staff were concerned that new products would rely substantially on state-of-the-art electronics rather than their primary area of expertise, mechanical engineering. Misperceptions due to lack of information about the projected nature of the changed state resulted in resistance, which took the form of reports on "why the goal cannot be achieved." Only when people acquired the necessary detail to fit themselves into the future scenario could they get comfortably involved in working to achieve it.

Reducing Employee Uncertainty

As in the previous issue, uncertainty about what will happen and when can cause increased anxiety and result in behaviors that work against achieving the desired end state. A natural human reaction to uncertainty is to "tighten up" and to seek answers, frequently within narrow circles of often uninformed but anxious colleagues, to what is happening and why. Rumors abound, fueled by speculation and largely erroneous, about future plans. Developing a detailed scenario of the future state provides information that at least suggests what will happen and clarifies the reasoning behind the change strategy.

Focusing Managerial Attention

Working on defining the future state diverts management's attention from dealing with the symptoms of current problems. It directs the energy of top management to setting out future organizational conditions that will eliminate the causes behind current symptoms and avoid new problems. Managers, especially in Western cultures, are generally rewarded for being "problem killers." The time orientation is short-term, and the preference is on a single-action solution: issue a directive, restructure a division, reassign a key player. Simply put, a premium is placed on identifying a quick "fix" for the problem, and action is generally focused on eliminating symptoms (and not necessarily causes). We have found that if top managers devote personal attention to long-range goals, describing in detail what type of organization they think is desirable, realistic, and attainable in the future, the insights they gain will lead to the development of more effective strategies and actions.

Case Illustration

In the midst of a major expansion plan, the chief executive officer of a large high-technology component manufacturer, known throughout the industry for producing high-quality components and consistently meeting promised delivery dates, found that product quality had been slipping significantly over the past two quarters. At weekly meetings with the general managers of the decentralized product divisions, the CEO would always remind everyone of the importance of maintaining the firm's reputation for high quality, and would stress that all divisions were expected to give top priority to quality control. Once a month, just before the close of their accounting cycle, he would meet with each general manager individually to check whether targeted volume would be met and to put the "fear of——into any general manager who was not meeting shipment targets." Yet quality continued to slip over the next two quarters.

The CEO, to show that he was serious about the quality issue, instituted a corporation-wide "zero-defects" program and established a new vice-presidency for quality. However, quality assurance personnel remained under the control of the individual operating divisions. Every vice-president signed a written commitment to support the zero-defect program. The firm established mandatory training programs for manufacturing and quality control staff and even management personnel within the divisions. Still, over the next six months, quality remained below the level the CEO considered acceptable, even though it was slightly better than the average for the industry. Although growth in volume was proceeding in accordance with the corporate goals, the company's image as a high-quality producer was growing tarnished.

Not until one of the staff vice-presidents volunteered a personal assessment of why the quality program was not working did the chief executive learn that his own behavior might be at the root of the problem. The vice-president pointed out that while the CEO "talked as though quality should be everyone's top priority," his actions really communicated that (1) meeting volume targets and shipping dates were paramount in importance; (2) that quality improvement was not primarily the responsibility of manufacturing but rather of the quality control function; and (3) that the problem could and should be solved relatively quickly and simply. It was noted that the senior managers' bonuses were determined solely by their performance against meeting volume targets and shipment commitments. It was also pointed out the CEO had "absolved" sales and marketing, engineering, research and development, corporate support functions, and even, to an extent, the division general managers of any significant responsibility for product quality improvement. Finally, the CEO was made aware that making a high-quality product was no longer a source of pride among the bulk of employees, especially those hired during the recent expansion. Quality as such was no longer a part of the value system or culture of the organization.

The chief executive and vice-president spent the next few hours defining what the organization should look like in three years, "when quality is *the* core value of the organization and product quality is the distinctive characteristic of the company's market image." They redefined "quality" to include all tasks within the company, not just the manufactured product. They described a future state in which every individual in every function had personal quality targets and measures. Everyone would be a member of one or more "quality teams," both within and between functions, whose function was to analyze and modify operating procedures to improve quality. Quality improvement would be defined as an ongoing, continuously incremental *process* with the ultimate goal of zero defects. Quality measurements for individuals, functions, and divisions would be prominently posted. All improvement would be publicly recognized, and significant improvement at all levels would be financially rewarded. There would be no separate quality control division, as responsibility for quality rested with everyone. A corporate "school," with all executives serving as core faculty, would be created to support the change process through training and to socialize new employees.

When they had a fairly broad description of the desired future state, the CEO remarked, "Over the past year I considered nearly all the things we've just described and rejected them all because no single action would achieve the kind of quality improvement that I wanted." By engaging in an effort to define, in

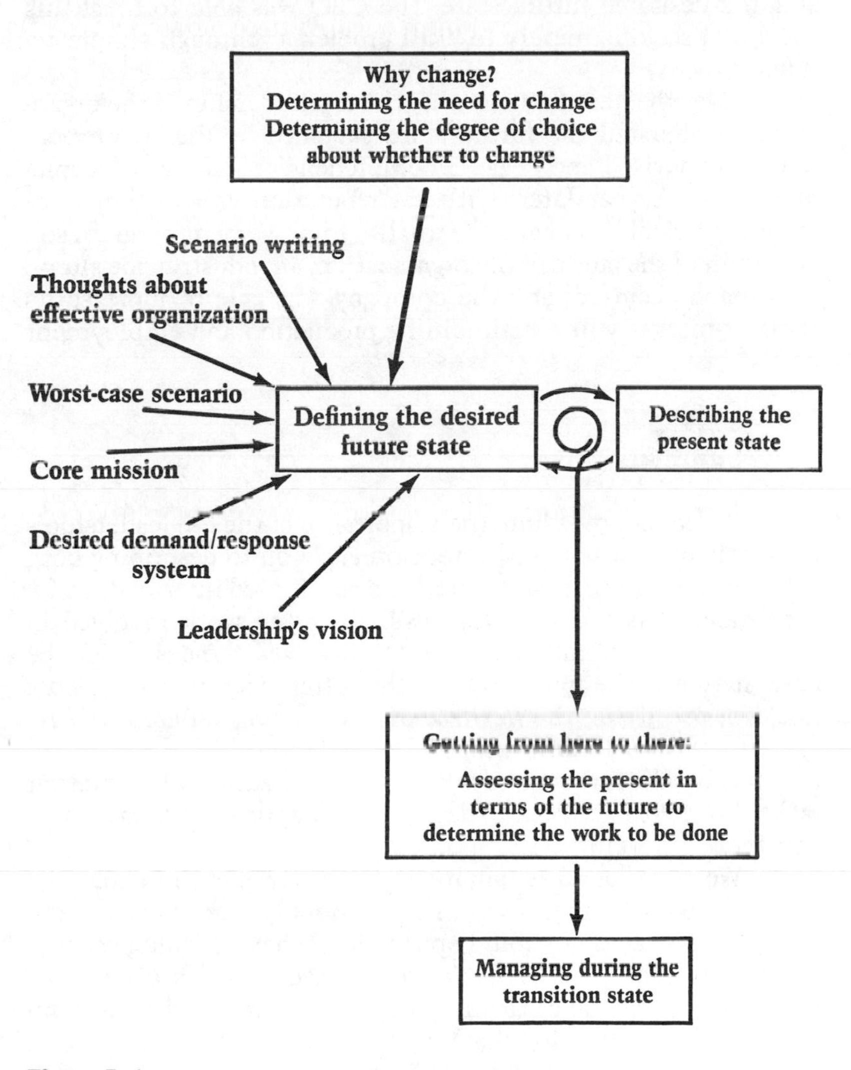

Figure 5–1
Defining the Desired Future State

detail, a desirable future state, the CEO was able to break his pattern of seeking merely to "kill problems" through simple actions.

Over the next few months, the top leadership of the organization elaborated the future state sketched by the two executives, and devised and began a comprehensive strategy of implementation. A year later, with its reputation as a high-quality producer reestablished and the quality improvement program solidly a part of the fabric of the organization, an industrywide slump in demand occurred, and the company was able to increase its share of market while maintaining production and employment levels.

Summary

We cannot overstate the importance of the top leadership's giving significant personal attention *early on* to describing both the oganization's ultimate vision and the desired intermediate future state(s). As Figure 5–1 shows, all of the work involved in describing a "desirable future state" involves choices about the basic nature of the institution in the future. Identifying the *core mission,* specifying the *desired environmental demand and response systems,* defining *corporate values and vision,* and determining the elements of an *effective organization* all represent tasks that are too critical to delegate to staff or subordinate managers.

We have found it helpful to forget temporarily about the present situation and describe, in behaviorally prescriptive detail, how the organization should appear and behave at some specific point in the future. This *written scenario* provides a vivid description that can be critically analyzed, and which directs managerial attention to achieving long-term goals for the organization rather than solely responding to immediate problems.

6

Assessing the Present

Benchmarks for Change

Defining the Present State

So far we have studied the sources of the drive for organizational change, managerial choices in responding to those forces, and the need to define a realistic and desirable changed organizational condition. The actual changes required to attain the future state have only been *implied* to this point. It is critically important, however, that management be *explicit* about its strategy for managing the transition. As in any decision-making process, the better the input information, the more likely the decision will be appropriate and effective. Earlier, we noted the need to develop a clear picture of the present state. Defining the *need for change* and determining the degree of *choice about whether or how* to change provide only a partial picture. Prior to making specific choices about change tactics and action plans, an *assessment of the present,* taking into account the desired future state, must be completed.

It is important to take a detailed look at the present system before determining an action plan for achieving future goals. Organizational managers often make erroneous assumptions about the current state of their organization when they are developing change strategies. If this happens, subsequent action plans are likely to be confused and prone to frustration; the change managers will experience unexpected resistance, and probably fail to achieve the desired future state.

To guard against such an outcome, management needs to develop a clear, comprehensive, and accurate view of the current state of the system. What is needed is a detailed behavioral description of the system's organization — current and recent, formal and informal — and its relevant environmental relationships.

Methods of Picturing the Present State

Several methods can be used to produce this image of the present state. Managements often commission a major study of the current organization prior to goal setting in order to understand the nature of the problems it has perceived. The results of such studies can be used to develop the present state picture, if management is convinced that the information will provide an accurate assessment of the *current* situation. Another alternative is to bring together a team of people who are collectively informed about the current state of affairs by virtue of their day-to-day contact with all the relevant subsystems of the organization. This team can then develop an accurate and detailed assessment of the present state based on firsthand experience. Questionnaires, interviews, focus groups, and other means can all be useful in this work. The point is that it is crucial for management to develop an accurate and comprehensive picture of the organizational present. This image, when examined in light of the future scenario, permits the determination of *what needs to be changed* and *what does not need to be changed.*

Making a Diagnosis

Anyone who is managing a change and attempting to identify what aspects the present state needs changing must take the following diagnostic measures:

- Identify and set priorities within the constellation of change problems
- Identify relevant subsystems
- Assess their readiness and capability for the contemplated change

Let's look at each of these steps in more detail.

Constellation of Change Problems

Any change problem is made up of a cluster of possible changes. If you wrote down *every* problem that you felt could be associated with a change effort, the list would be as long as your arm. It would probably mix up "big" problems with "small" ones, many of them overlapping or interconnected. To sort out this complexity, it is useful to think in terms of clusters or *constellations of problems*. For example, there might be a constellation revolving around maintaining production, or one having to do with internal communications, or one concerning the development of required skills. It is recommended that you write a brief description of each major problem constellation you have identified. The description should specify the *who* (individuals and groups), *what* (organizational processes), and *how* (consequences) of the problem and its effects. Then examine all of the constellations together for any *domino effect*. Is there a certain key problem that must be dealt with before anything else can happen? Or are there smaller interconnected issues: if we change X first, will a solution to Y follow, or at least fall into place fairly easily? The results of this analysis will be helpful when you develop action plans for managing the transition state.

It is also useful to identify the *types of changes* that will be required in the various organizational processes. This analysis flows readily from a comparison of the future state scenario and the present state description. Areas of potential change include: attitudes and values, organizational policies, managerial practices, control and reward systems, technical skills, and the like.

Determining Relevant Subsystems

Another early step in defining the present system is to determine what specific parts of the "people system" are most significantly involved in the anticipated change process, and what changes in current attitudes, behavior, or work will be needed to reach the desired end state. This entails thinking about every aspect of the organization as it relates to the change goal.

We are talking about the *minimum* number of individuals or groups who must support the change or it won't happen. This is the "critical mass" needed for change to occur.

Individuals and groups within the organization that would be significantly affected by a change are not the same as the critical mass. Identification of these subsystems making up the critical mass is a first step in anticipating and preparing for resistance. Later we will discuss in some detail a process for fostering the commitment of key subsystems to the management's change goals.

Example. A large American manufacturing organization with plants in several countries intended to build a new European plant. Firmly committed to improving the quality of working life, the parent company had for a number of years conducted experiments in organizational design, which involved higher worker participation in the plants' management and new systems of pay, work design, and governance. Manufacturing the new plant's product would require advanced though already well developed, technology. The plant would open with an American management group at the top, but as soon as possible the plant would operate with an almost entirely indigenous management and work force.

In defining the desired state after the opening of the plant, the project management assessed the technical process of manufacturing the product, the physical environment in which the product would be made, and the cultural environment of the host nation, whose social conditions were very different from those of the country in which the parent company was located.

Critical Systems

Six critical subsystems were identified: (1) the manufacturing management, (2) the management group of the country in which the plant would be located, where there were already some ongoing activities, (3) the plant manager, (4) the operating management group, (5) the first-line leadership, and (6) the managers' families.

This set of systems grew out of an analysis of both the future and present states with the change strategy accomplishing the following large goals:

- Teach the new technology to both the Americans and the management group from the host country
- Create a new community in which people from both nations could work together in the host country
- Develop a common technical language for the host country and the home office
- Ensure a relatively comfortable living environment for workers and their families
- Find a mechanism to deal with cross-cultural issues

Appropriate systems to target for change, then, may include the entire organizational hierarchy or only pieces of it, both inside and outside the formal structure. A conscious identification of the subsystems primarily affected by a particular change helps to clarify directions for the strategy.

Determining Each Subsystem's Readiness and Capability for Change

Assessment of the *readiness* of the various subsystems for change requires an analysis of the attitudes of these systems toward the change. In the example above, the management's assessment covered many areas: the preparation of the manufacturing management for this major experiment, the readiness of the American plant managers to engage in a nontraditional process, the attitudes of the recruits for management positions in the host country toward relocation, the families' attitudes toward this major disruption in their way of life, and so forth.

In addition to the attitudes of those involved, the *capability* to make the change should also be examined. Whereas *readiness* for change has to do with willingness, motives, and aims, *capability* involves power, influence, authority to allocate resources, and the possession of information and skills required to carry out the necessary tasks. Let us suppose that the training manager in an organization feels a strong need to introduce a program to develop middle managers. Such a program needs organizational approval and the support of both the top executive officers and the line general managers in order to be really viable. The training manager should consider the various subsystems — the chief executive, the line managers, and the middle managers who would be involved in the program — to determine which ones to analyze for readiness and capability to change. The training manager too might be a relevant subsystem.

Having identified the relevant systems, the training manager would then measure the individuals' readiness and capability for the anticipated change. For example, the assessment that the personnel director is strongly enthusiastic about and supportive of the program would be rated as *high readiness.* By contrast, the chief executive might feel that management training is an acceptable but low-priority activity, and that it certainly should not tie up major financial or human resources. This attitude would be considered *low readiness.*

On the capability measure, however, the personnel director might have no budget to support the program, whereas the chief executive officer could easily release the necessary funds. Thus the chief executive officer would have *low readiness* and *high capability,* while the personnel director would have *high readiness* and *low capability.* In developing a strategy for change, the training director would have to find a way either to increase the readiness of the chief executive, in the hope that he or she would then release the funds, or to increase the capability of the personnel director to provide the resources necessary to support the program.

We have found it helpful to use a simple chart to assist in the assessment of readiness and capability, as in Figure 6–1. Although the resulting analysis is still rough, it can help focus attention on the areas that must be worked on to create the critical energy needed for change to occur.

Having determined the readiness and capability of critical subsystems for the particular change, the next step is to find ways of increasing the readiness and capability of the organization as a whole. Some of the considerations are as follows:

In the left-hand column, list the individuals or groups who are critical to change effort. Then rank each (high, medium, or low) according to their readiness and capability with respect to the change.

	Readiness			Capability		
	High	Medium	Low	High	Medium	Low
1.						
2.						
3.						
4.						
5.						
6.						
7.						
8.						
9.						
10.						
11.						
12.						
13.						
14.						
15.						
16.						
17.						
18.						

Figure 6–1
Readiness Capability Assessment Chart

1. If traditions, norms, and ways of work are firmly entrenched, some "unfreezing" intervention will be needed to break people away from their deeply held attitudes or behaviors and ready them to try something new.
2. If the priorities or the goals of the organization are perceived very differently within the various systems, effective change can take place only if a goal-setting exercise or process is undertaken to build a consensus.
3. Structures probably need revision if the organizational chart does not reflect the change tasks to be done.
4. Some temporary systems and projects may need to be set up if present structures are unable to institute the change.
5. Some educational activities may be called for if new information, technical knowledge, or skills are required to achieve the change conditions.

Case Illustration 1

Background. A company that manufactured materials-handling equipment purchased a small electronics company that designed both the software and hardware of computer systems for running materials-handling vehicles. The "cultures" of the two organizations were complementary but very different. The parent company was a third-generation, family-managed, single-technology organization, situated in a small town where it was the dominant employer. The new firm was located several thousand miles away, in a large industrial park in California. Staff members of the old company were conservative, old friends, and second-generation employees. The personnel of the acquired company were technical people, entrepreneurs, "modern electronics" scientists, and other types regarded as prima donnas.

Economic conditions indicated that the activities of the two companies should ultimately be integrated. The executive management was faced with the choice of whether to (1) bring the new enterprise into the old physical setting, (2) operate them as two separate enterprises with a liaison group, or (3) work in a project organization. The leadership also needed to determine what management structure and information systems must be developed. Should these two companies be two separate profit centers with general managers? Or should the acquired organization be an arm of the technical function of the parent company?

Diagnosis. The top management of the parent company, in collaboration with the leadership of the acquired company, did an analysis along the lines indicated on page 64, and reached the following conclusions: (1) Traditions and norms were found to be heavily locked in for the old company, not at all for the new company. (2) Goals were not clear and universally shared between the two organizations. Employee goals in the acquired company were invention, improved state of the art, entrepreneurial development, and get-rich-quick, whereas the goals of key personnel in the old company were stability, moderate growth, and other traditional values. (3) The corporate structures were not found to be frozen in old ways, but as is they were certainly inappropriate to the task of integrating the two technologies. (4) The need to set up one or more project systems alongside the current operation was acknowledged. It was agreed that there certainly was a need for a project organization to manage the integration of the two technologies. Further, it was decided that a project organization should probably be developed to study resource allocation between the two organizations, and that a project system might be needed to manage the entire enterprise. (5) New information, technical knowledge, and skills required to achieve the change condition were deemed both available and integrable. The view was that some specialized technologies should remain separate, but other parts could be combined.

Strategy. From this diagnosis, top management developed the following strategies:

1. Do not start with physically integrating the two institutions.
2. Develop a project organization, with the technical leadership of both institutions collaborating on specific areas of technical and product integration.

3. Create a management structure for the project organization such that the head of the acquired company is its chief operating officer. Locate the executive function in a group composed of the chief operating officer, the vice-president of technical services, and the vice-president of operations from the parent company.
4. Work through the goals issue by having a significant group of the leadership of the acquired organization attend the parent company's management meetings.

This is a brief illustration of how assessing readiness-capability issues enabled an organization to determine managerial strategy.

Case Illustration 2

Background. The leadership of a nursing college decided to make a major change in the way its curriculum was organized and nursing was taught. The impetus for the change was the increased diversity of nursing graduates' first jobs in recent years. The current curriculum trained nurses to treat patients in hospitals, but did not place much emphasis on teaching them about family treatment, ambulatory care, community delivery settings, and other outpatient situations.

From a series of studies, the faculty concluded that the best way to redress this imbalance was to change the organization of the curriculum from subject areas or disciplines, such as medical-surgical nursing or community nursing, to types of patient care, specifically, "primary care" (continuing and preventive treatment), "secondary care" (a more continuing backup type of chronic care), and "tertiary care" (acute care in a hospital). It was decided that each of the three one-year curricula should focus on one of these major styles of care, and that the various disciplines — medical, surgical, psychiatric, and the like — should be slotted into this format.

Although there had been general faculty agreement on the necessity for this change in order to meet the changing external demands, there were obviously all sorts of mixed and negative feelings as well among members of the faculty about loss of control, status, and teaching quality. The dean's original strategy for managing the change had been to appoint a group of committees — mostly younger faculty who advocated the change — to do some planning of the new curriculum. Initial efforts had moved very slowly for a variety of reasons: reluctance of department heads to provide the time for junior faculty to work on the project, different degrees of commitment or motivation, and general overwork and overload of activities within the present curriculum.

Diagnosis. The dean was rather frustrated with the progress of the change. An analysis of the situation elicited the following answers to the questions listed on page 64: (1) The various systems and groups needed "unfreezing" in light of the strong traditions and norms in operation. (2) Goals were found to be generally shared, but means and priorities were widely differentiated; some process for setting priorities would probably be required. (3) Structures were frozen in old ways; the new situation would definitely require structural reorganization. (4) There was a project system — the curriculum-planning groups — already in force alongside the current operation in order to institute the change; but it was not working well. Diagnosis seemed to indicate the need for a whole new management system for the transition period, during which the old curriculum and the new curriculum would be conducted side by side. (5) New educational skills would clearly be required to achieve the change. The new curriculum called for team teaching, a process with which most of the faculty was inexperienced. In addition, the fieldwork involved in the new curriculum would be very different from the traditional hospital practice of the past; new supervisory techniques would need to be learned.

In weighing these various factors, the dean and her advisers recognized that of the various conditions, an "unfreezing" intervention to make the entire faculty aware of the organizational issues would probably need to precede any other activity. Some sort of activity was needed that would allow the entire faculty to participate in defining what kind of management would be necessary.

Strategy. The dean began by convening a one-day workshop for the entire faculty. Outside experts from a nearby management school presented to the group an overview of the process of organizational change. They outlined some of the inherent problems in change, the need for and some methods of doing organizational diagnosis, techniques of analyzing the forces involved in an organization and for developing a strategy, some understanding of the difference between the old and new state of affairs, and the need for a management uniquely designed to govern the transition state.

A written case, which looked strangely similar to their own school, was presented to the workshop members to "solve." Participants were divided into small, maximally heterogeneous working groups composed of older faculty, new faculty, department heads, and program heads. The groups were asked to analyze the "case school," develop a strategy for managing its transition to the new curriculum, and be prepared to advise the dean on how to manage the change. Then a representative from each subgroup reported its findings to a role-play dean (the real dean was in the room).

This simulated "confrontation" with the real situation made the entire faculty aware of the total situation and the problems involved. Everyone recognized that a management structure would need to be set up to manage this interim period.

The second major element in the strategy involved the determination of a structure for managing the transition state. Coordinators for each of the three curricula were selected from senior faculty by the dean, with the support of the functional department heads. Each coordinator headed a curriculum development committee, whose members were appointed by their department heads. The task for each committee was to produce the curriculum for its area, even though its members would not necessarily be teaching the courses.

The third part of the strategy was the development of a coordinators' group, headed by the curriculum coordinator for undergraduate programs. This group reported directly to the dean and paralleled the existing hierarchy of department heads. Mechanisms were instituted for handling conflicts over priorities. Team-development activities were instituted for helping the new

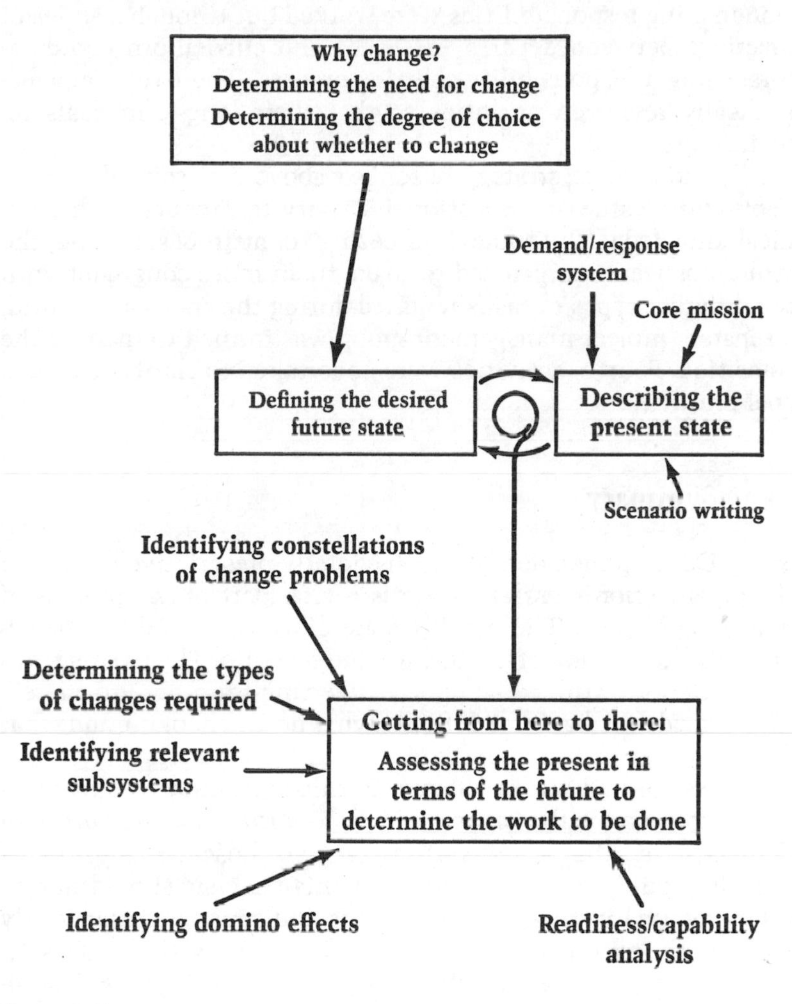

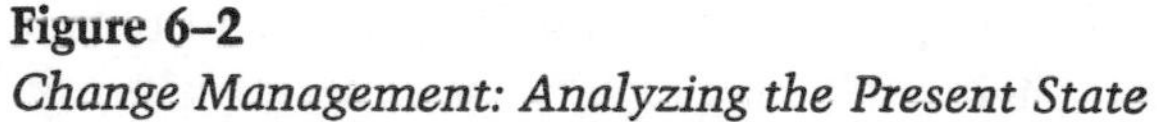

Figure 6–2
Change Management: Analyzing the Present State

curriculum and teaching teams get established effectively. Decision-making responsibilities were worked out through a series of meetings between department heads and curriculum coordinators, using a responsibility-charting process. The two groups periodically reviewed priorities so that their long-term goals remained clear.

The change strategy described above had several components. First came an educational activity to produce both technical knowledge and some "unfreezing" of attitudes. Second, the structures were reorganized to make them more congruent with the different types of tasks required during the transition. Third, a separate project-management group was formed to manage the transition. Fourth, activities were undertaken to clarify goals and goal priorities.

Summary

Developing a detailed, behaviorally prescriptive picture of the organization's *present* state is a vital part of the process of managing change. The present state diagnosis should be developed *after* definition of the future state scenario. The two pictures determine the work to be done in "getting from here to there"; they provide the basis for defining what needs changing and what doesn't.

As pointed out in Chapter 2, this preliminary work must take into account the organization's *core mission,* the *nature of demands,* and the *patterns of response* to those demands. However, it should be remembered that this analysis should not be solely focused in the past and present, but must simultaneously consider the executive management's long-term vision and its detailed scenario of the desirable future condition. Figure 6–2 summarizes various considerations in analyzing the present in terms of the desired future. Such analysis clarifies the remaining work required to move the organization through the transition state. It provides the data needed for informed choices about action taking.

7

Getting from Here to There

Transition Management

In any change there is always a future state — a place or condition one wishes to achieve; a present state — the current condition in relation to the desired state; and a *transition state* — the getting from the present to the desired state: the period during which the actual changes take place.

The tasks and activities of the transition state may or may not look like those in the future or present states. In managing the overall change process it is always important to (1) determine the major tasks and activities for the transition period, and (2) determine structures and management mechanisms necessary to accomplish those tasks.

For example, if one decides to build a new plant to boost the manufacturing capacity of an existing product, the end state is obvious: new plant; good technology; efficient, low-cost operation; good place to work. The management structure and style is less obvious — either similar to or different from present plant management, depending on the change goals. Management — or the existing hierarchy — is the present state. The time period from the decision to build (on a piece of land) to the opening of a fully operating plant is the *transition state.* How should that be managed?

In today's manufacturing world, it is highly unlikely that the existing hierarchy would directly manage the transition state. The leadership would more probably set up a "plant start-up team" consisting of operations staff, such as the plant manager-designate, and representatives of resources such as engineering, information, and personnel. The team would plan the work flow, manage it throughout the transition stage, and do the final design of the operation and task activities. In Chapter 8 we present a case study of a complex change, which addresses these points in more detail. For now, we want to focus on two aspects of transition management: *activity planning* and *management structures.*

Activity Planning

An *activity* or *change plan* specifies the critical activities and events of the transition period: when first moves will take place, when meetings will be held to clarify new roles, what information will be communicated to whom on what day, and when the new structures will start to operate.

The activity plan is the road map for the change effort, so it is critical that it be realistic, effective, and clear. The following are five characteristics of an effective activity or change plan:

- *Relevance:* activities are clearly linked to the change goals and priorities
- *Specificity:* activities are clearly identified rather than broadly generalized
- *Integration:* the parts are closely connected
- *Chronology:* there is a logical sequence of events
- *Adaptability:* there are contingency plans for adjusting to unexpected forces

Two considerations in devising an activity plan deserve

specific mention: determining where to focus initial attention, and selecting specific change technologies.

Where to Intervene First

Having determined what needs to be changed, the manager is now faced with the choice of where to concentrate his or her initial attention. Any of the following subsystems of an organization can be considered as a starting point for a change effort:

- *Top management:* the top of the system
- *Management-ready systems:* those groups or organizations known to be ready for the change
- *"Hurting" systems:* a special class of ready systems in which current conditions have created acute discomfort
- *New teams or systems:* Units without a history and whose tasks require a departure from old ways of operating
- *Staffs:* subsystems that will be required to assist in the implementation of later interventions
- *Temporary project systems:* ad hoc systems whose existence and tenure are specifically defined by the change plan

Looking back at our earlier cases, we can see that all of the choices made took into account the issue of starting point. For example, in the illustration of the materials-handling organization (pages 64–66), early intervention was made at the top of the system through a change in governance, whereas the creation of temporary systems was an early step in the nursing school case (pages 66–70). Early interventions effected by management personnel upon the entire system can be a good preliminary alternative to working with specific subsystems, such as the group of advocates ready for the change or the new coordinator groups. Unfortunately, however, there is no "cookbook" — no surefire, predetermined solution. Our argument throughout is that if one asks questions systematically, one is likely to come up with better judgments and better choices than otherwise.

Choosing Intervention Technologies

In addition to figuring out where to start, another issue for analysis involves finding a way to move the change process forward. We have already introduced some possible techniques: using an educational activity as an intervention, redesigning a structure, or creating a new change management system.

In targeting an initial intervention, one must identify the most promising early activities and carefully think through their consequences. Some of these activities might be:

- An *across-the-board intervention,* such as the faculty meeting in the nursing school
- A *pilot project* linked to the larger system, to try something out in one area as the first of a number of projected changes
- *Experiments,* which differ from pilot projects in that they may or may not be repeated to test different types of interventions
- An *organizationwide confrontation meeting* to examine the current state of affairs, such as the senior management conference in the electronics firm[1]
- *Educational interventions,* as in the nursing school case
- Creating *temporary management structures,* as with the nursing school and the materials-handling company

One general point to remember is that *it is most difficult for a stable organization to change itself,* that is, for the regular structures of the organization to be used for managing the change. It is often necessary to create *temporary* systems to accomplish the change, as seen in practically every case illustration above. Effective change effort often requires new ways of approaching problems; existing mechanisms may be inappropriate or ineffective in such situations.

We also strongly recommend that the choice of technology for managing the change be a later rather than an early decision.

[1]Richard Beckhard, "The Confrontation Meeting," *Harvard Business Review* 45, no. 2 (March–April, 1967): 149–55.

All too frequently, this is the first decision made by the management. We often hear from a management trying to institute a change: "What's needed here is a planning exercise" or "We've got to have a management by objectives system" or "We need a management-training program." We are suggesting that those decisions are of relatively low effectiveness and somewhat high risk, unless they are related to and grow out of the issues discussed earlier in this chapter.

Transition Management Structures

If the transition state is very different from either the prechange or the postchange condition, a separate management structure congruent with the tasks and organization of resources within this unique state will be needed. Imagine, for example, the replacement of a manual bookkeeping system with a computer-based electronic data-processing system. There are three sets of conditions: (1) those that existed before the change, (2) the condition that will exist when everything is on the computer and working properly, and (3) an intermediate condition that will exist as the computer comes on line and gets debugged, jobs change, and people learn new ways of working. This last condition — the transition — has people working in relationships different from those of both the past and the future.

The critical question confronting the executive manager is: How should this time of transition be managed? Should the person in charge of the old bookkeeping operation supervise the change in terms of allocating work, rewarding people, and determining timetables for going on the electronic system, or should the person who will run the new system be in charge during the transition period? Or should both people be in charge, or their common supervisor?

There is no cut-and-dried answer. The most appropriate management system and structure for the ambiguous transition state is the one that creates the least tension with the ongoing system and the most opportunity to facilitate and develop the new system. For example, in trying to implement a new curriculum design involving different responsibilities, allocations of resources, and assignments of teachers, one would probably find a time during which the old curriculum was being taught under the old structure and the early parts of the new curriculum were being brought into the program. Again, a critical question facing the manager in this case would be who should manage the change — the department heads who ran the old curriculum, the program directors for the new curriculum, a special projects manager, or the dean.

A successful transition manager usually has the following attributes:

- The *clout* to mobilize the resources necessary to keep the change moving; in a change situation, one is often competing for resources with others who have ongoing work to do
- The *respect* of the existing operating leadership and the change advocates; a great deal of wisdom, objectivity, and linkage may be needed in order to make balancing decisions, such as how many resources to put into the new activity and at what pace
- Effective *interpersonal skills*; a large part of leadership at these times requires persuasion rather than force or formal power

Various types of resources and mechanisms are appropriate to transition management, depending on the nature of the change and the anticipated problems. But whatever the choice, making and communicating explicitly the leadership's decisions about the transition management structure are important for effective transition.

Alternative Structures for Managing the Transition

The Chief Executive. The head of the organization takes responsibility for coordinating the change effort. For example, in the development of a new plant, the plant manager may personally function as project manager for the change; if this requires considerable energy, the day-to-day operations of the present state may be delegated to others on the CEO's staff.

The Project Manager. The executive manager may temporarily give either a staff person or a line person the executive power to manage the change. Here, the project manager functions not from his own base but from the executive manager's office. This alternative is very similar to that of a product manager in a technical organization. The product manager is a program integrator charged with the responsibility of getting the job done, but having to do so with resources whose "homerooms" are in other parts of the organization.

The Hierarchy. The supervision of transition management is given as a separate or additional responsibility to the regular operations managers. These individuals are thus "job-enriched," with explicit new responsibilities different from their usual operating duties. An example can be drawn from an organization that is moving from a functional to a matrix structure in order to improve interdepartmental integration and coordination for new-product development. In carrying out the transition, the heads of technology, marketing, and manufacturing would hold monthly meetings with newly assigned product managers to make companywide decisions about new-product possibilities. For the functional heads, this type of activity would differ from their usual responsibilities: they would be a management committee functioning as a new-products committee.

Representatives of Constituencies. Here the change management structure is a group that represents the major constituencies involved in the change. For example, the implementation of a new system of employee-management work relationships might be managed by a group representing both employees and managers. If one is moving toward more participation and democracy in working conditions, one might want representatives from blue-collar workers, technical and administrative junior management, senior management, and top management to monitor, oversee, and manage the change.

"Natural" Leaders. Sometimes the executive manager selects a group whose members have the confidence and trust of large numbers of their colleagues, even though they may not be official representatives. For example, change in a medical school would probably be facilitated by securing the commitment of the heads of medicine, surgery, and perhaps one or two other departments; then other departments and suborganizations could "deliver a constituency."

The Diagonal Slice. This alternative serves the need to get continuing input from many different levels, cultures, and functions within the organization. The diagonal-slice mode involves getting a *representative sample* of the various functions, locations, and levels, as opposed to *formal representatives of groups.*

The "Kitchen Cabinet." This American expression refers to those colleagues (or sometimes cronies) with whom the executive manager consults on an informal basis, but who in fact have high influence on both the executive manager and the organization. Most chief executives have two or three internal colleagues whom they trust and consult in this manner. The kitchen-cabinet alternative may be the optimal mode for the executive manager who wishes to maintain direct control over the change, desires objective and candid input from others in the organization, and yet is concerned that line managers may have a vested interest in various options that distorts their input.

To summarize: the executive manager should (1) define the transition state as a set of conditions separate from both the present state and the future state; (2) determine what type of governance or management would be most effective; (3) set up such a management structure and system; and (4) communicate the existence of this structure or system to all relevant parties. The transition is facilitated in most cases by having a management system for the transition state that is separate, or at least uniquely distinguished, from both the present state of operations and the future state of affairs.

Case Illustration 1

In a large hospital, patient care was coordinated by interns who had responsibility for a number of patients in widely scattered areas of the hospital. The interns and residents on the medical ward felt strongly that individual patient care would be improved if the coordination were put more into the hands of the nurses, who were each assigned to a specific geographical area with a fixed number of patient beds. It was not proposed that nurses take over doctors' technical responsibility, only that the *coordination* of care could be better handled by the people who were in physical proximity to the patients. The residents also suggested that wherever possible, patients assigned to any one intern should be located together in the hospital.

This proposal for a change in patient-care coordination (grouping interns' patients) was sent up through normal administrative channels. The chief of medicine, to whom residents reported, approved the implementation of the proposal on an experimental basis. The director of nursing, to whom the nurses reported, gave tacit approval. The hospital director was notified of the experiment and gave his blessing. The chief of medicine assigned responsibility for the management of the transition to those interns and residents who wished to participate in this experiment and bring about this change. The experiment was approved by the hierarchy, but the transition management was in the hands of the advocates — only a minority of all the residents on the medical service.

When the change was initiated, the residents encountered terrific resistance throughout the hospital. Orderlies would not do the rearranging needed to concentrate all of an intern's patients in the one area; instead, the young doctors moved beds. These relocations caused general chaos throughout the hospital — in the patient-reception area, the telephone department, the billing office, and other units. Administrative staff threatened to strike, and other residents joined in the general resistance to the disruption. Many staff members felt that the change negatively affected patient care. The hospital director had to step in and renew his support of the experiment to keep it going. But since residents rotated through units on a monthly basis, a new group soon came onto the medical ward and immediately went back to the old system.

The experiment itself, as seen by doctors, nurses, social workers, and certain patients, was considered very successful in terms of patient care and satisfaction. The disruption caused by the differential work patterns, however, was more than the system could handle without adequate preparation; so at the first opportunity, the system reverted to its old condition. The problem might have been alleviated or even overcome if a project management group, coordinating the changes from the chief of medicine's office, could have conducted the experiment two or three times, maintaining a careful liaison with the most heavily affected parts of the hospital system — the administration and support services. However, there was no such appropriate transition management, and the experiment failed.

Case Illustration 2

A company was making a major change in the relationship between its sales and manufacturing functions and in the control of manufacturing schedules and priorities. The company was part of a complex organization making products for several different business areas. Its current-state system was something like a job shop: the various product groups submitted their requirements for the product, including an estimate of market needs, to the manufacturing managers, who then used a formula to allocate how much of what product would be produced in which plant during the following work period.

The practice had resulted in skewed inventories, delays in delivery, and a number of other dysfunctional conditions. The general manager of the operation decided that it was necessary to create a distribution department — a new management structure that would take the market demands, determine the manufacturing requirements necessary to meet those demands, schedule the production requirements into plants in different parts of the country so as to optimize distribution of the products, and relay all this information to manufacturing management.

The change plan was simply to add the new distribution department to the general manager's staff. The change was explained to everybody, and the various functional heads were asked to work out the implementation. After a month or so it became apparent that the change had produced increased confusion because of new reporting lines (warehouses now reported to distribution rather than to plant management), new roles, and changes in territory and "turf." The general manager sensed that the three functional heads (sales, manufacturing, and distribution) would be unable to work together to operate the changed condition. He created instead a new management committee, with himself as chairman, composed of the head of manufacturing, the head of distribution, the coordinator of field warehouse operations, the

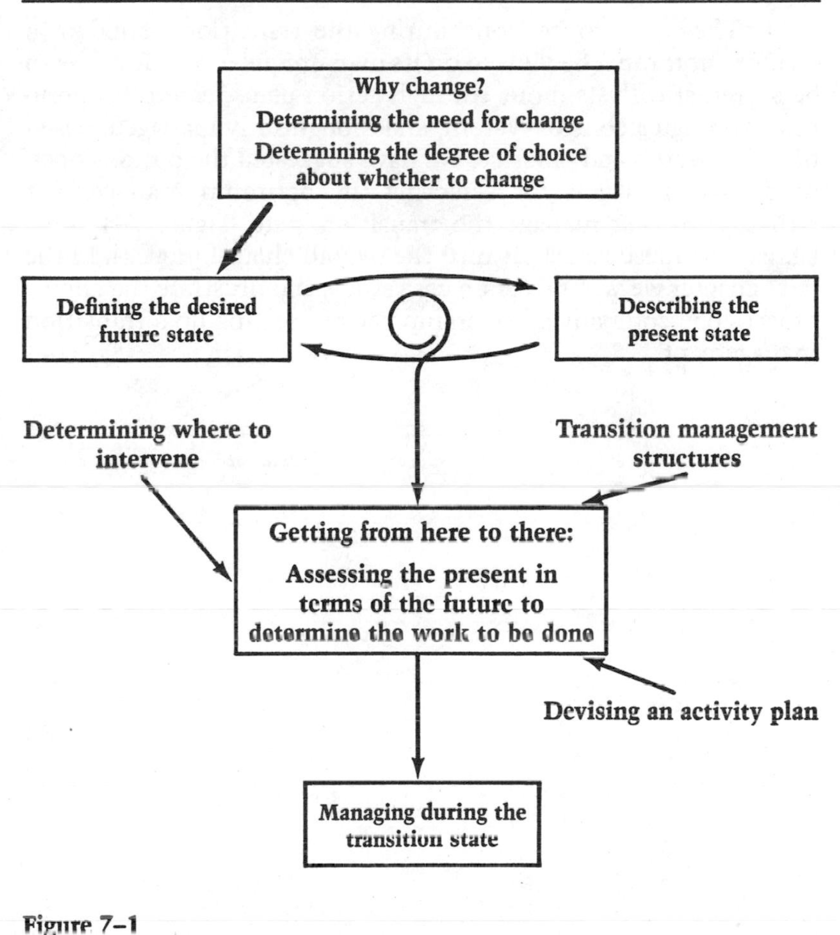

Figure 7–1
Change Management: Managing the Transition

production scheduling czar for manufacturing, and a marketing analyst. This group became the "general management" overseeing the change. The carefully chosen combination of people and the clout of the general manager's office worked to ensure the success of the change effort.

Summary

The work to be done during the transition period of a change effort must be viewed on its own unique terms. It needs to be systematically laid out through action plans, carefully monitored through a control system, and thoughtfully managed. Based on our research and practice, we have suggested the options open to change managers for selecting the optimum management structure to best manage the transition state. Figure 7–1 illustrates how these issues fit into the overall change process. In the next chapter we will present a case study, and illustrate the choice process one company's leadership used in setting up a transition management.

8

A Case Study

In this chapter we want to describe a complex change in an organization where the management consciously used a change model to move from one set of conditions to another. We will briefly outline the situation and then try to illustrate how the approach we've been discussing in this book was used by one organization.

Background

Company X had a very successful fifty-year tradition of producing a popular consumer product. The quality of the product had been so good and their market position had been so dominant over many years that the name of the firm and its primary product were synonymous in the public's mind. The company made a basic product with a variety of applications, and distributed the product throughout the world. Its sales were well over $10 billion and its profits had been consistently high throughout the company's lifetime.

Competition in the product line came mainly from other American concerns, although in recent years the Japanese had become increasingly important competitors. German and English producers had also begun to encroach on the market share. Competitors, however, had not been able to provide the wide range of quality products and related consumer services that this company had provided due to its superb distribution system and its highly centralized manufacturing.

Recent Background

Now that there were worldwide competitors, the quality and price of competitive products had begun to threaten the company's position. The fundamental principle in the company's strategic posture was to maintain market share. This priority now for the first time began to demand price adjustments. Since the organization had operated on a relatively basic formula over the years, price changes materially affected the heavy manufacturing and other overhead factors that had been quite adequately funded in the past.

The *organization,* obviously, reflected the stability of years of preeminence and profitability. The organization promoted from within, and most of its employees had never worked for any other organization. The firm's "cultural" traditions were therefore firmly established and fully respected. The organization was paternalistic, taking very good care of its people. Its compensation was way above market and local community rates; the benefits programs were among the best; it was a comfortable place to work, and offered exciting advantages to those who were involved in technical innovation. The combination of high pay, promotion through the ranks, and virtual lifetime employment kept employee turnover low; virtually all those who achieved top positions in the organization had come up through similar backgrounds.

When the competitive position changed and dominance of the price factor emerged, it became clear that the company could not continue to hold its market share unless major, perhaps even radical, organizational changes were introduced. It became the mission of the leaders of the various segments of the organization to find ways of "working smarter": becoming leaner and reducing overhead.

Our case is concerned with the manufacturing complex of

this organization. As mentioned, the manufacturing was quite centralized, with most of the product developed and produced for worldwide distribution at one giant manufacturing establishment. This plant had well over 30,000 employees, and was clearly the principal employer in the city where it was located.

To meet the changing requirements imposed by the outside environment, it was going to be necessary to change many work practices, substantially reduce personnel, and find new manufacturing methods that significantly increased productivity.

Given the ironclad rule that the company must maintain its standards of product quality, the new business objective became *low cost/high quality*. This represented a drastic change in the ethos of the organization. For example, it had been a tradition since the founding of the company that in order to protect quality and ensure productivity, virtually all raw materials were produced internally rather than purchased from suppliers. This resulted in significant cost inefficiencies, but tradition dictated that that was the way to do business. All such traditions would have to be reexamined if the company were to make a successful change.

The plant's organization was directed by a plant manager who was a vice-president of the corporation. Two deputies were also part of the leadership group, and beneath them were four major functional directors. Under them were plant superintendents, assistant superintendents, division or department managers and assistants, supervisors and team leaders, and finally operators or technicians (see Fig. 8–1).

Diagnosis

Determining the Need for Change

The need for change was obviously initiated by the competitive situation. The plant manager recognized that, just as in the rest of the organization, there was no choice of whether or not to make the change, but only how. The initial diagnosis of change imperatives was that the firm needed to cut personnel numbers by a significant amount, and so the first structure for managing the change was set up on the assumption that a reduc-

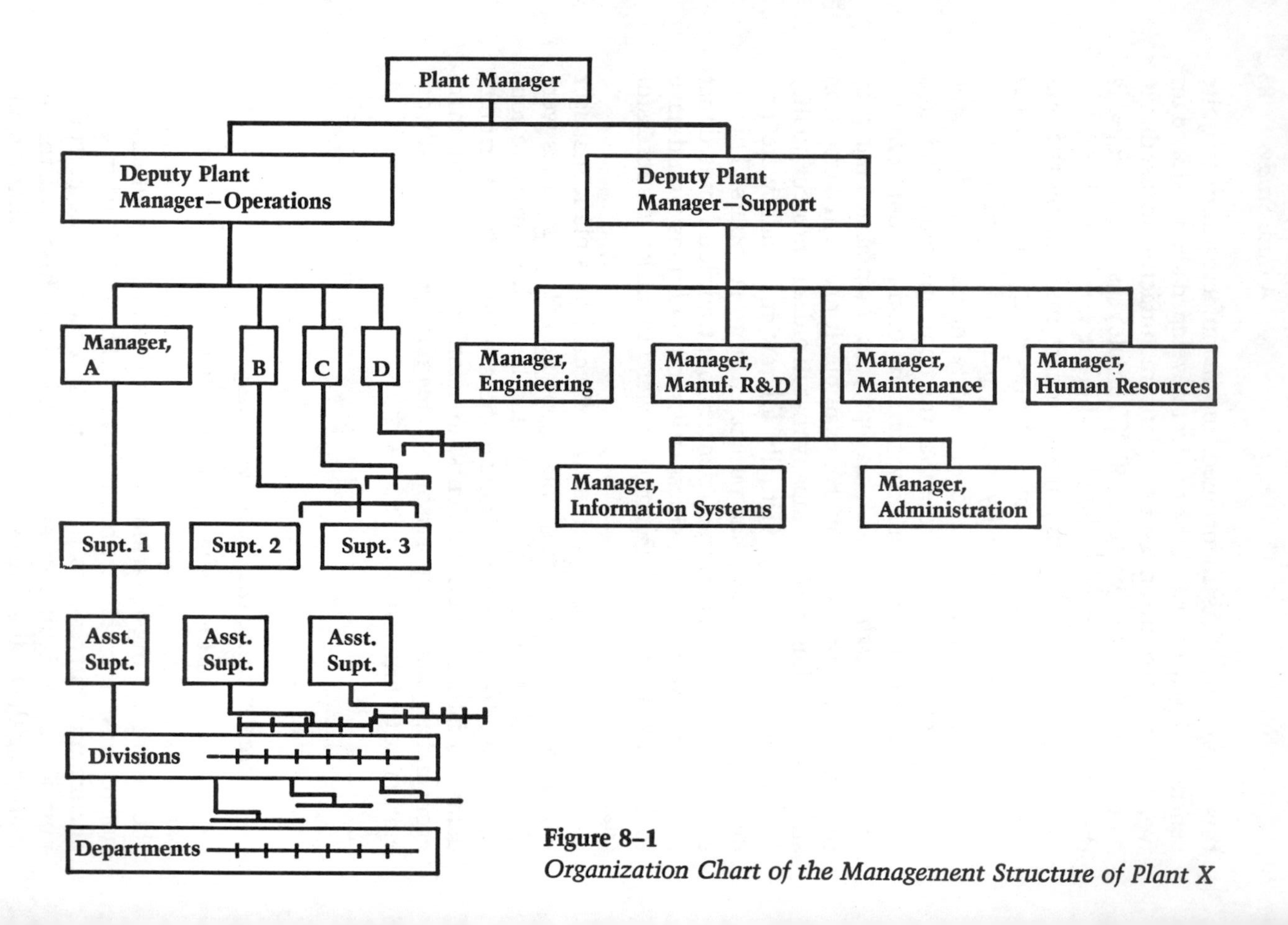

Figure 8–1
Organization Chart of the Management Structure of Plant X

tion in force was the *change problem*. As the top management pursued the issue, it became relatively clear to them that the change problem may have been miscast.

Defining the Future State

As the leadership began to define their vision of the manufacturing system — one that would beat the competition — it became quite clear that the significant change would be a change in the *way work was done*, and a reduction in both personnel and others costs would come about as a *corollary change*. Once the problem was *redefined*, partly through an analysis of the present condition but largely through the development of a set of objectives and a vision for the future state, the managers then decided on a different system for managing the change process.

The Present State

In examining the company's current patterns of work organization and exercise of authority and control, it became clear that the existing functional organization was built on the classic manufacturing mode, with the plant being a cost center not closely related either to marketing or to the customer. It was recognized as well that operating middle managers were fairly traditional and set in their ways, though successful and financially well off, due to the policies of the company. The top management of the plant recognized that this group would probably be quite resistant, consciously or unconsciously, to any dramatic change, particularly since productivity and output could not be sacrificed and therefore could not share the pinch of any change efforts.

The managers also recognized that the comfortable, stable character of the organization would severely undermine efforts to operate leaner or give up things, unless the employees could join with the management in recognizing a common "enemy" — in this case, outside competitors.

The managers' revised first major move was to increase employee discomfort with the present state; to show that the present modus operandi could not continue if the company was to maintain its market position. The theme that was communicated was that they all had to work smarter and more effectively and in this process there would be redundancies and changes in ways of work.

The plant management developed a few assumptions that would serve as guidelines for whatever change activity was developed. First, they set as a goal the elimination of all "assistants." This would cut out several layers of management, and would communicate to the entire organization that overhead was what had to be cut or modified first and that workers on the job would therefore be doing much more "managing" of their work. Top management also recognized that resources for contributing to the change were widely distributed, and that it would be necessary to tap these resources if significant efficiency were to be achieved while maintaining quality.

Organizing Change Management

Recognizing that there probably would be great difficulty getting the present top operating managers to function as managers of the change, top management decided to bypass them and to create a parallel temporary body to manage the change to the new condition. One of the top executives was selected to be the czar of the change effort. A group of younger, upper-middle managers from various parts of the system was chosen as a full-time "effectiveness team"—the top management of the change effort, working under the leadership of the "czar." These men and women were high-potential, high-energy people who were well aware of the challenges, and were also somewhat dissatisfied with the present method of doing business. Their *transition management plan*, or grand strategy, was the following:

Step 1. The members of the team went out into the field and collected, through questionnaires and interviews, a list of areas of potential improvement throughout the plant organization. They got about 150 suggestions of ways to do things better.

Step 2. An arbitrary limit of fifteen priority items was set by the effectiveness team. After analyzing the 150 ideas, the group chose fourteen.

Step 3. Small groups, each headed by a member of the effectiveness team, were appointed to study each item and recommend the organizational design and structure for the new way of operating. These teams met for anywhere from a month to six months, depending on the problem, and produced biweekly interim reports for the effectiveness team, who could thus keep track of the entire effort. Each study team was given a target date to complete its work.

Step 4. When the study teams reported — first to the effectiveness team, then to the top manufacturing management, and in some cases even higher in the corporation — decisions were made to go ahead, or refinements were made that led to such decisions. For each go-ahead decision, a *transition team* was formed. The mission of this team was to manage the work of the transition — getting from here to there; to create a specific design for the future state; and to set the timetables for the myriad changes involved in any one large transition, such as moving buildings or restructuring job roles, or in the people area, providing a period just before the changeover for either early retirement with a very good sweetener, or continued service in the organization.

These transition teams operated for six months to a year. Each one was headed by somebody who was in a key position for that particular function or set of functions. The transition period leader might or might not become the operations leader when the change took place. Many people on the transition teams knew that their own current assignments would be eliminated in the process of change but they were heavily committed to designing and planning the new condition.

As the effectiveness team's work was handed over to the transition teams, the new *management of the transition* became the transition managers as a group, which then could study the interrelationship of all the changes.

Results

The organization was able to effect approximately a 20 percent cut in personnel. It made a significant reduction in production costs, both by cutting staff and by converting a number of previous "make" activities to "buy" activities. The organization disengaged from a number of traditional functions, particularly overhead, and productivity rose significantly.

Summary

The purpose of this case study was to demonstrate the step-by-step process of managing complex change: starting from the future state, defining the change problem, studying the constellation of problems to be managed, setting priorities, examining the present state and resistance to change, and designing a management structure that could manage the transition. This systematic approach to managing a complex change provided the desired results, with no loss in the quality of the product and a remarkably small loss in morale. Much of the negative energy that existed at the beginning of the change was converted into positive energy toward improvement. Those who would perhaps suffer or lose job titles because of the change were aware of the alternatives; that is, that the business could be in deep trouble. They accepted the necessity of belt-tightening and put their energy to more creative ways of becoming more productive.

We move on now to examine the issue of getting the commitment of the people needed to direct, manage, and participate in a complex change. We will look at the process of getting commitment, the defining of a critical mass, and strategies for securing commitment.

9

Commitment Planning and Strategies

Readers are familiar with the expression, "The best laid plans of mice and men . . . " The same applies to a change effort: the "best laid plans" will not ensure the desired change unless one has the *commitment* of whatever critical mass is necessary to ensure the achievement of the goal. The planners must determine who in the organization *must* be committed to the change and to carrying it out for the change actually to take place. Traditionally, managements consider issues of commitment from a political stance, saying that they "have got to get a few people on board," "need the chief executive's approval," or "have the majority of the engineers going along." We suggest here that in addition to one's intuitive political judgment about who needs to be "committed," there should be a systematic analysis of the system to determine those subsystems, individuals, and groups whose commitment to the idea, to providing resources (money and time), and to carrying it out and persevering with the new process is necessary. Membership in these groups may vary.

Critical Mass

As we have described earlier, in any complex change process, there is a *critical mass* of individuals or groups whose active commitment is necessary to provide the energy for the change to occur. It is impossible to quantify the number of people or the roles necessary to make a critical difference. For example, Ralph Nader and a few lawyers became a critical mass in affecting business enterprises and their practices. In "forcing them" to commit and carry out changes one can, however, analyze the organization's systems that are affected by and effect the change, and judge the size of the critical mass for a particular change effort. It may be small, but it is nonetheless vital.

To give one illustration, the chief executive of a large, complex organization became aware of the need for closer contact between the top-management committee and the division managements. When executives joined the management group in the corporate headquarters, they tended to become isolated from the operating divisions and from the field. This tendency promoted autonomy and decentralized control of activities, but made it hard to gather adequate information about staff members' attitudes toward their working conditions and other issues.

The company's management had been surprised by an attempt to organize junior middle management. The chief executive officer had subsequently made an extended "sensing trip" throughout the system, listening to employees at all levels and ranks talk about their conditions. He had spoken to his colleagues on the management committee about the need for better communication, but not much had happened. The chief executive diagnosed the desired change as a strengthening of contact between members of the central management board and the general managers of divisions. He realized that the critical mass for making such a change would be four or five key members of the twelve-person corporate management team. Those four or five executives had been with the company a long time and had always been the norm setters; if they now changed their behavior, they would carry along their fellow management-committee members.

The CEO developed a strategy for getting those key members to introduce new ways of behaving toward the field leadership, the division general managers. He knew that it was also necessary for a significant number — perhaps half — of the general managers to support the change effort. The general managers had to be made aware of their own need for better information about what was going on in their own divisions concerning such issues as work conditions; in addition, they would need a system for reporting their findings to the executive board or central management. For both the executive board and the division general managers, there was an identifiable number that made up a critical mass. Having targeted the critical mass, the chief executive could then make a specific plan for getting both his board colleagues and the general managers involved.

Commitment Planning

A *commitment plan* is a strategy, described in a series of action steps, devised to secure the support of those subsystems which are vital to the change effort. The steps in developing a commitment plan are:

1. Identify target individuals or groups whose commitment is needed.
2. Define the critical mass needed to ensure the effectiveness of the change.
3. Develop a plan for getting the commitment of the critical mass.
4. Create a monitoring system to assess the progress.

Commitment Charting

Various techniques can be used to get the commitment of target individuals or groups identified as the critical mass. One method that has been developed for forming a diagnosis and action strategy to get the necessary commitment is called *commitment charting.* This technique works on the already stated assumption that for each member or group in the critical mass, it is necessary to get some degree of commitment, or the change won't happen; but the level of commitment need not be the same for everyone. A simple rating has been developed with three kinds of commitment:

Let it happen
Help it happen
Make it happen

It is sufficient to get the *minimum* commitment judged necessary from each individual or group; don't expect every member of the critical mass to be ready to "make" the change happen.

To make a commitment chart, list all the members or groups who are part of the critical mass — those whose commitment is absolutely essential — on the vertical axis of the chart. Across the top, list the degrees of commitment: "No Commitment," "Let it happen," "Help it happen," and "Make it happen," and draw vertical lines to make columns (see Fig. 9–1).

For each member or group in the left-hand column, place an O in the box that indicates the minimum commitment you must have for the change to occur. Do not try to get as much as you can; settle for the least you need.

Then study each of the people and groups as they are *now* and, using your best judgment, put an X in the box that represents their *present* degree of commitment.

Where the O and the X are in the same box, circle them and breathe a sigh of relief: no work to do to get the necessary commitment.

Where the O and the X are *not* in the same box, draw an arrow connecting them. This gives you a map of the work to be done (though not how to do it) to get the necessary commitment.

Strategies for Getting Commitment

Now that you know what commitment you need, the next question is, how do you *get* it? In addition to power or persuasion, there are a number of possible *intervention strategies* you can employ to create the conditions for commitment.

Often, when people are not committed to the degree re-

Key Players	No Commit-ment	Let It Happen	Help it Happen	Make It Happen
1.		X →	→	→ O
2.		X →	→ O	
3.		X →	→	→ O
4.		O ←	← X	
5.			(XO)	
6.	X →	→ O		
7.		X →	→	→ O
8.		(XO)		
9.	X →	→	→ O	
10.			O ←	← X

Figure 9–1
Sample Commitment Chart

quired by the change effort, they are resisting in some way. Where resistance exists, it is necessary to work with it and honor it, but also to find ways to neutralize it for short periods so that the resister can hear your perspective on the problem. The following *intervention strategies* can help you overcome resistance:

- Problem finding
- Educational intervention
- Resistance management
- Role modeling
- Changing reward systems
- "Forced" collaboration

If the degree commitment requisite to a change effort is not there, we must assume that there is a *resistance* to the change. Resistance is a normal part of the change process; in fact, there can be no real change without some resistance. Resistance is also an *attitude,* usually a fixed bias or "frozen" position. To eliminate resistance, one must "unfreeze" it by creating a situation that is *neutral* — one in which existing attitudes are not challenged but rather clarified, without anyone's being forced to take positions on them.

Problem Finding

Problem finding is one such neutral mechanism, by which those concerned with change get together to identify and clarify all aspects of the problem. Problem finding allows players to change their minds without having to say so. It also allows people to listen to each other — temporarily — without having to screen what they hear through their own biases. It assumes that the very process of clarifying an issue or problem, as opposed to problem solving or action taking, will be unthreatening enough to encourage commitment.

There are several important rules to remember in problem finding, all of them aimed at limiting the sense of risk among the participants:

- It must be *bounded.* The activity can only be for the purpose of problem and issue identification; *no action is allowed.*
- It must have a *minimum of structure.* There must be a clear willingness to limit the work to clarification, but within that framework the exchange of ideas should be as free as possible.
- It must have a *minimum of public output.* There need be no minutes, and certainly no public statement of consensus or agreement.
- It must be *temporary.* An ad hoc requirement is important.

Case Illustration

A large consumer organization with diversified activities and decentralized functional organizations was operating on several conflicting philosophies relative to staff development, compensation, and other organizational improvement processes. The overall treatment of personnel was being handled from several different points of view, to the detriment of recruitment efforts in the marketplace. Attempts to find creative and human solutions to this problem usually met with resistance; turf issues tended to mount, and departments viciously protected their own systems and traditions.

Some members of the personnel development division, having heard about problem finding, decided to try this low-key technique to deal with the problems of "how we treat people." They formed themselves into a steering committee (although nobody knew what it steered). The ground rules were that the personnel development staff would invite selected individuals to the first meeting, whose sole agenda would be to decide whether there was anything worth meeting to talk about. The invitees represented a cross section of hierarchical levels, functions, and operations. The first meeting group included the chiefs of personnel, engineering, and management systems, the head of all technical organizations, the vice-president of research and development, two organization development consultants, a trainer from sales, and a staff person from marketing.

It was established that membership in this "nonorganization" would be defined by attending meetings; additional members would be invited by the standing group and uninvited, if necessary, at a subsequent meeting. The ground rules were that no decisions could be made; the group could issue no statements; no member could say anything that was defined as a group decision or consensus; no minutes or records of meetings would be kept; and each meeting would be an ad hoc event (although, in a single concession to structure, the group agreed to meet every three months on company time). The stated reason for the group's existence was to define issues and problems and clarify what the issues were. The group was in no way allowed to *solve* anything.

From the first it became clear that the group had a powerful impact on policies and practices. For instance, at one meeting an archaic practice of differentiating summer payments for different types of students was brought up for the fiftieth time. A senior vice-president in attendance said, "Do we do that? Why do we do that?" He was told that the personnel department (whose leadership was also at the meeting) was stuck on this policy, that it had been a tradition nobody was willing to change. The senior vice-president said, "I don't understand why we do that. I'm having lunch with ——, who heads all services, including personnel, and I'm going to ask why we do that. It doesn't seem to make any sense."

One week later, the policy was changed. This is not an isolated example; rather, it is typical of the kinds of things that can be done to "thaw" the system through this particular type of intervention.

Educational Intervention

Just as problem-finding activities are designed to unfreeze attitudes, so are *educational interventions.* The operative concept here is that there are two places inside which the activities of our daily lives are irrelevant: the house of worship and the school — or, more broadly, the learning situation.

In the classroom, it usually doesn't matter who you are the rest of the time; all students are equal during class. For improving communication skills, it is irrelevant what students do in their professional and private lives; they're all here to *learn.*

Educational activities for managing organizational change can help people understand a change problem and offer needed commitment.

Resistance Management

We have already said that resistance is normal and to be expected in any change effort. Resistance to change in organizations takes many forms; change managers need to analyze the type of resistance in order to work with it, reduce it, and secure the needed commitment from the resistant party. A useful formula for thinking about the resistance process is:

$$C = [ABD] > X$$

C = Change
A = Level of dissatisfaction with the status quo
B = Desirability of the proposed change or end state
D = Practicality of the change (minimal risk and disruption)
X = "Cost" of changing

Factors A, B, and D must outweigh the perceived costs (X) for change to occur. If any person or group whose commitment is needed is not sufficiently dissatisfied with the present state of affairs (A), eager to achieve the proposed end state (B), and convinced of the feasibility of the change (D), then the cost (X) of changing is too high, and that person or group will resist the change.

Case Illustration

A division president of a large multinational organization was very anxious to change the approach to doing business in his organization from a technology-driven and manufacturing-driven to a more marketing–customer-driven enterprise. His entire management consisted of long-term staff who had come up through the technical ranks — including the marketing people. They all considered the quality of the manufacture of the products to be more important than worrying about markets. Given changes in market demand, this was no longer an accurate assumption.

The chairman met with all his key leaders and very clearly indicated the necessity of shifting the company's focus. All of the top management expressed support for the change and agreement on its desirability. A few changes in reporting lines were made. A global change strategy was developed.

But not much happened. The managers, consciously or not, were resisting both the effort involved in rethinking how problems should be solved and the upheaval of restructuring business teams composed of marketing, manufacturing, and other groups. As a result, very little changed in the first few months.

The chairman, who had from other experience become acquainted with the resistance theory, met with his personnel and organization management staff to diagnose the attitudes of all the key members of the organization according to the C = ABD formula. They found that some of the key managers simply were *not dissatisfied enough* with the status quo. Evidently, the chairman's earlier sales pitches had not been taken seriously enough; an intervention was needed to increase their discomfort with the current situation. Other managers, especially in manufacturing areas, approved of the change on an intellectual basis, but did not see the desirability of the end state as furthering their personal interests; they needed a different kind of intervention. Those few who were dissatisfied and also envisioned the change as desirable were concerned that the first steps would so upset the unions or the management practices that there would be a big problem; a third intervention was necessary for this group.

By sorting out the key players and thinking through which of the issues — dissatisfaction, desirability of the end state, or practicality of the first steps — was critical for each key player or group, the top management and the chairman were able to develop custom-built strategies that reduced resistance and helped them move toward their desired change.

Role Modeling

There are times when commitment can be achieved only if it is seen as required, or if the leadership "practices what it preaches" by clearly demonstrating its own commitment to the change. One way of sending this message is for the norm setters (organization leaders) to incorporate change activity into their *personal behavior.* The norm setters thus provide *role models* for other members of the organization, demonstrating that "this change activity has priority; it is as relevant as our operating responsibilities."

Case Illustration

An organization operating in a fast-moving high-tech world was experiencing tensions between the scientific and technical personnel, on one hand, and administrative and the support staff on the other. Various kinds of training and development programs had been instituted, but they had not made a significant improvement. The chief executive of the organization was rather insulated from the daily events of the company and would only get feedback on the situation when a crisis arose. Certain staff members warned the leadership of the poor conditions; but when the top leader checked with his immediate subordinates, he was assured that everything was under control.

The situation was growing acute; the organization was about to lose some very useful and important resources. The director of human resources convinced the CEO to institute some "sensing meetings," informal talks with personnel at all levels that bypassed the organizational hierarchy. These meetings would probably yield information that would be significantly helpful in dealing with the technical–administrative rift. The chairman, who was concerned about staff communications, agreed readily. He told his management group that he planned to initiate a biweekly one-hour sensing meeting, in which he would listen to the concerns of various groups, and asked them to help set up a design so that each of these meetings had a different cross section of the organization — a group of secretaries from throughout the organization, a six-level vertical slice within one department, a diagonal slice, or a group of professionals. There was, of course, initial resistance and concern on the part of some executives reporting to the CEO, but they all agreed — however reluctantly — to the process.

The chief executive began holding the meetings, reporting back his findings to his immediate subordinates after each meeting. He established a firm ground rule that no manager could be punished for any mistakes that were exposed in the sensing meetings. During the first six meetings a great deal of information emerged that the president was able to pass on, without recrimination, to the top management staff. In addition, he was able to demonstrate, by his own behavior, the value of listening to people at all levels of the organization.

It did not take very long before general managers of divisions and departments started using similar techniques to get closer to their own people. The morale issues receded dramatically during the first few months, and stayed down for as long as the meetings were held.

Changing Rewards

A powerful way of reinforcing a change in priorities is to change the reward system. Too often, organizations encourage resistance by maintaining a reward system that is inconsistent with the new state of affairs. For example, if you want your employees to be more innovative, but you maintain a financial reward system and an appraisal procedure that only reward concrete results or meeting quotas (thus implicitly punishing "mavericks"), don't be surprised to find a fairly high resistance to innovation, and a credibility problem to boot.

The current literature is full of illustrations of the impact of changing reward systems. More and more companies are attaching rewards to the output of ideas or participation in improvement ideas. For example, the 3-M reward system for innovative ideas has significantly increased the creation of new and imaginative products in that organization.

The *ideal reward system* strives for a balance between rewards for what a person knows and for what he or she does. This system is out of balance in the hiring of graduates and master's degree students for industry, because they are rewarded much less for what they do than for what they know in their initial jobs. Conversely, in traditional manufacturing organizations, people in the workplace are rewarded disproportionately for what they do, and very little for what they know. Most new plants and organizations that are trying to develop better quality of work and working life are changing the reward system to one in which there is a better balance between the value of what a person knows and the value of what he or she does.

Case Illustration

The reward system can be defined by giving punishments or withholding rewards as well as by giving rewards. In one organization that had five related businesses — including cat food, dog food, and people food — the general managers of these businesses were in competition with each other for store shelf space and for getting internal manufacturing resources in order to meet their marketing and manufacturing quotas. The managers were rewarded for meeting their quotas through bonuses which, at the discretion of the president, could reach a significant figure — sometimes larger than the manager's actual base salary.

The president wished to find ways by which the different food divisions could provide synergy toward collaboration, such as combined advertising programs. He instituted a Monday morning meeting for business development and business planning to explore these issues.

General manager attendance at these meetings was laissez-faire, to use a nice word for it. The managers always found reasons for arriving late, leaving early, and not having done their assignments. Then at one meeting, the president announced to his colleagues: "You might like to know, now that it's bonus time, what criteria I will be using next week in deciding your bonuses. Sixty-five percent of your bonus will be based on your operational performance, as always; 25 percent will be my subjective evaluation of your contribution to our business planning; and the other 10 percent will be the degree to which you are creatively and actively working on the development of your staff, which has been indicated as a corporate priority."

The behavior of the division managers changed very dramatically at the subsequent meeting. Nobody was late, nobody left early, everybody had done his or her work, and the quality of their output improved significantly.

"Forced" Collaboration

Within an intervention strategy, it is often necessary to develop some low-risk mechanism or activity that allows people to collaborate even if they have vastly different biases. This only works, however, when there is already consensus on a bigger objective, within which disagreements over lesser issues can be explored.

Much change takes place at the interface between departments, between merging organizations, and through internal reorganization. Wherever the change brings the units of a larger whole into a new or different relationship, such questions arise as: "Who should act upon whom?" or "How should each party behave under the changed circumstances?"

Traditional ways of dealing with this issue are:

1. *Write new job descriptions.* This approach makes the assumption that the conditions of and relationships between job roles are always the same regardless of the tasks to be done. The reality is that tasks change and location of authority shifts depending on the tasks. In a certain situation, position A may be "supporting" position B; change the task and it may be B supporting A. They're the same two positions but different relationships depending on the *task* or *work.* For example, under one condition manufacturing staff might be the "performers" and marketing personnel the "supporters," whereas in other circumstances it might be exactly the opposite.
2. *Let the boss decide.* This alternative is usually less than satisfactory. Bosses are usually chosen as decision mak-

ers because of their higher position in the power structure — not because they have more information than the subordinates. Letting the boss decide is a waste of management time and energy, because if an organization is trying to push decisions down to the lowest level where sufficient information occurs, having bosses mediate issues between two subordinates does not add any information to the situation but involves a third party simply on the basis of power.

3. *Applying the "expert" solution,* consultants or experts providing the "proven" solution. This can often provide useful guidelines; but the expert solution that may work in one place doesn't necessarily apply in another place or another situation.

All three of these alternatives operate from the standpoint of defining the "roles" of interacting parties. A more productive way of approaching the problem, we believe, is to find out the *behavior* desired. To do this, one needs to define the optimum behavior for each of the several roles that affect a particular decision or action.

Responsibility Charting

A technique called *responsibility charting* has been developed to assess alternative behaviors for each party in a series of actions bringing about a change. Each actor in a particular decision is assigned one of several behaviors for each step in the change process. A person might be the "project manager" for a particular action, or perhaps only an approval source; one might have to provide active support or resources for a certain action, another simply may need to be informed or consulted before the action is taken.

A description of responsibility charting follows. We then offer a few illustrations of how the technique has been used.

Making a Responsibility Chart

Responsibility charting clarifies behavior that is required to implement important change tasks, actions, or decisions. It helps reduce ambiguity, wasted energy, and adverse emotional reactions between individuals or groups whose interrelationship is affected by change. The basic process is as follows:

Two or more people whose roles interrelate or who manage interdependent groups formulate a list of actions, decisions, or activities that affect their relationship (such as developing budgets, allocating resources, and deciding on the use of capital) and record the list on the vertical axis of a responsibility chart (see Fig. 9–2). They then identify the people involved in each action or decision and list these "actors" on the horizontal axis of the form. Actors can include:

A = Approval (right to veto)
S = Support (put resources toward)
I = Inform (to be consulted before action)
— = Irrelevant to this item

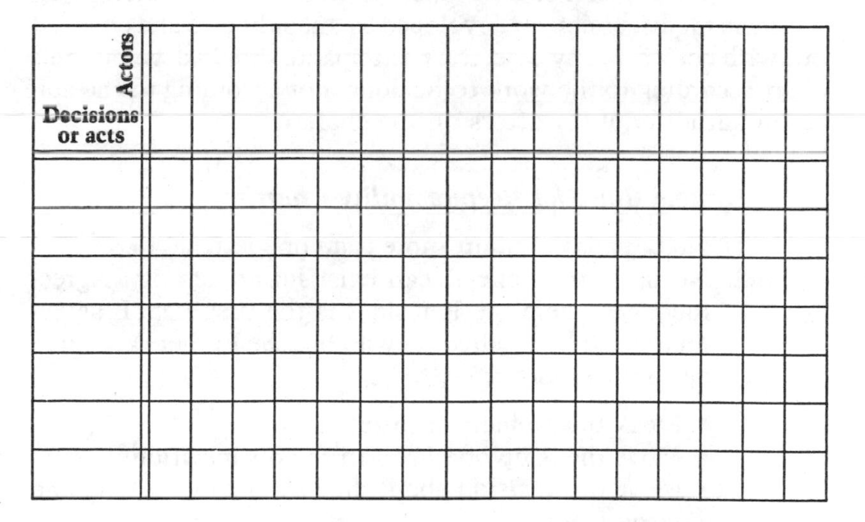

Figure 9–2
Responsibility Chart

- Individuals directly involved in a decision
- Bosses of those involved
- Groups (board of directors, project team)
- People outside the organization (union official, auditor, banker)

Finally, the participants chart the required behavior of each actor with regard to any particular action or decision, using the following classifications:

R Has *responsibility* for a particular action, but not necessarily authority
A Must *approve* — has power to veto the action
S Must *support* — has to provide resources for the action (but not necessarily agree with it)
I Must be *informed* or consulted before action, but cannot veto
— Irrelevant to the particular action

Applications

Figure 9–2 can be developed by leadership and then given to others for discussion, or developed by subordinates and checked out with bosses. In any case, the participants should develop their chart according to the work to be done, not according to the status or authority of the actors on the chart.

Ground Rules for Responsibility Charting

1. No box may contain more than one letter.
2. No more than one R can exist for an activity. Agreement on where the R resides is the first step. If agreement can't be reached on who has the R, there are three options to follow:
   - Break the problem into subparts
   - Move the R up one level in the organization
   - Move the *decision* about the location of the R up one level
3. Once the R is placed, other letters can be agreed upon, with the ground rule that no box contain more than one letter.

4. Avoid assigning too many A's; it leads to great difficulty in obtaining a decision. Renegotiate to change some A's into S's or I's.

The group that develops the chart should test it out with any actors not present during its production. Preferably, no major actor should be absent. The participants can also use the completed chart to check expected behavior and to call attention to others when their actual behavior falls out of line with the consensus noted on the responsibility chart.

The usefulness of responsibility charting lies not only in the end product of an agreed-upon chart but also in the new understanding and appreciation of people's roles and required behavior that grows out of the charting process.

Some Further Guidelines

1. If an item has several A's — say, one R, six A's, one S, and one I — it will undoubtedly be very difficult to accomplish that task. For example: one organization decided to increase its benefits plan for management. The change was agreed to at all levels of the organization; the board approved it; and the compensation staff was directed to implement the plan. Nine months later, the plan was still not in. A responsibility-charting exercise indicated that each of the organization's major profit centers had assigned itself an A because it was an independent profit center accountable to the center for meeting its budget. Because this new program required the investment of funds that were not budgeted, each profit center's manager felt it was his or her choice to decide whether or not to start the program this year or next year.

The managing director pointed out that because the board of directors was the source of the change, S, rather than A, was really the appropriate symbol for the profit center's role. It did not take long for the profit center managers to agree, and then the program was instituted very quickly.

2. If a second-rank manager fills out the chart, one might find a skewing of A's under the senior executive. Subordinate managers tend to give their bosses more A's than the bosses in fact want.

3. The decision about who assigns a letter to a role can be tricky. In one situation, for example, the management group of

an organization decided that first-line supervisors in the production department should be held accountable weekly for financial issues, such as scrap losses, and should also receive timely information about their progress toward certain financial objectives. However, the controller's department, which was part of general headquarters, refused to develop a new cost-accounting system for the production department. The current accounting systems focused primarily on the needs of the top officers of the organization and the tax accountants; and another system would have to be added in order to provide this new type of information for production. The controller's department felt that as the top financial resource, it should have responsibility for deciding whether or not such a system, with the attendant costs, should be introduced.

At a responsibility-charting session, it became clear that the controller's department defined itself in the A category, whereas others lower in the organization felt strongly that the department should have an S — that it should be required to produce the system. The general manager supported those who were arguing for the S, on the basis that the task required it. This ruling changed the basis for making decisions from hierarchy position to task accomplishment.

Further Applications

Case Illustration 1: A Change in Structure. A large consumer company identified with a particular selling strategy decided to change the strategy. Previously the company had sold its product, which was used in interior decorating, through specialty stores. Long known as a single-product firm, the company now wanted to establish itself as a decorating company. This entailed changing the products in the stores, changing the relationship of the franchised stores to the corporation, differentiating the various types of buyers — housewives, contractors, and so on — and providing outlets for the customers' new needs.

The prechange organization was a marketing–sales–functional structure. All sales were handled within geographic regions under the direction of division managers, reporting in turn to regional sales managers. Plants made products on demand for the various regions, and the technical-service unit made special blends of products as required by the sales division.

The company's top management felt that a new organizational structure was needed to fit the new marketing plan and corporate image. Accordingly, the sales department was maintained, but purely as a selling organization. Product managers were created within the marketing organization and were given worldwide responsibility for sales development in their particular product or market area. Also created were product-technical managers, who came from the technical organization but also had a product or business orientation. Members of the technical-service staff would now receive all of their instructions from the product-technical director, rather than from the sales division.

Everyone in the organization, with the exception of the production and finance divisions, now had a new role, a new set of task responsibilities, and new relationships. Rampant confusion was to be expected.

The strategy for dealing with the confusion was to conduct a series of responsibility-charting conferences. The first two-day conference focused on the employees holding new roles — the product managers from marketing and the technical-product managers — and the top executives of the organization, namely, the directors of marketing, manufacturing, technology, and finance and the group vice-president.

After opening remarks by the vice-president, the participants proceeded to do a responsibility-charting exercise. They identified areas of necessary decisions and activities, made a list of the actors, and then assigned behaviors to them. Because the top managers of the organization were also participating, the assigned behavior could be "reality-tested" right then. The output of the two days was a map of the general modus operandi, as seen by the top management and the occupants of the new roles.

At the next conference, the two sets of roles in marketing — sales and product management — and the two sets of technical roles — product management and technical service — met in order to work through mutual responsibilities and to assign behaviors for their roles in the new setup. Difficulties that had arisen with the earlier models and maps were now resolved by the top-management group, which had also attended the first workshop. The revised models were then distributed throughout the organization and became the basis for implementing the change.

The change, a massive one involving several thousand managers, went smoothly into effect; employees were operating in their new roles within six weeks of the announcement of the change. The process of having all of the key people sit down together and develop the new modus operandi was credited with having significantly enhanced the efficiency of the change.

Case Illustration 2: An Interface Problem. The regional headquarters of a major oil company had been working for a few years on developing a new type of franchise relationship with some of the company's gas station owners. The problem was complex, and there had been all sorts of misunderstandings, conflicts, slowdowns, and differences of emphasis between staff areas. The top management — the managing director and the directors of marketing, operations, and finance — were concerned about this issue because it was a matter of significant investment and cost; but they had been unable to resolve it.

At a periodic meeting one of us held with this group, they mentioned the difficulties they were having with this particular franchise problem. It was suggested that they do a responsibility-charting exercise on the problem, which they did. As a result, they discovered that they did *not* have a consensus about the location of different types of responsibilities and behaviors. This problem was relatively easy to work through.

By coincidence, the next day one of the authors was conducting a development meeting with the operating management (about forty people) of the same organization. As part of the content of the meeting, the consultant described responsibility charting and suggested that the group do a responsibility-charting exercise on the franchise case, with which they were all very familiar. The participants were divided into eight groups, all of which were to work on this problem. The groups came up with different results, although the patterns were similar. It struck the consultant as significant, however, that practically all of the patterns were different from the one that the top management had produced the day before. It then was suggested that the group meet with a member of the top group to compare notes on the respective results of their exercises.

From this meeting, several things became obvious: (1) there was a gap in communication between hierarchical levels; (2) the involvement of the top management was needed to expedite the change; and (3) the distance between top management and top operating management was dysfunctional for issues of this kind.

Faced with the objective assignment of behavior in the responsibility charting, all the managers were able to treat the franchise issue as a problem rather than as a question of management style or role conflict. The problem on which they had been working for two years was resolved in four weeks.

Case Illustration 3: Responsibility Allocation. In a large medical school, the teaching curriculum had been organized by discipline, such as biochemistry, medicine, or surgery. Students took courses in the various technologies, in addition to their fieldwork.

The faculty decided to incorporate into the discipline-based curriculum some core courses, structured around types of patient care delivery. In this type of course, the teaching faculty came from a variety of departments, such as pediatrics, medicine, psychology, and psychiatry.

As the program directors appointed for the core program began recruiting faculty for their courses, they encountered considerable resistance from some of the department heads. Both groups, feeling considerably frustrated, brought a number of their problems and differences to the dean.

In their search for a better way of resolving these kinds of issues, the key program directors and department heads were exposed to the responsibility-charting technique. In a two-day exercise, they worked through the responsibilities and the assigned behaviors of each role as it related to the handling of faculty assignments, rewards, changes in curriculum, and other factors. The result was to significantly reduce the dean's arbitration activity, clarify decisions for the total faculty in various areas, and provide agreed-on methods of operation for handling these types of issues.

It has become increasingly clear that when interface

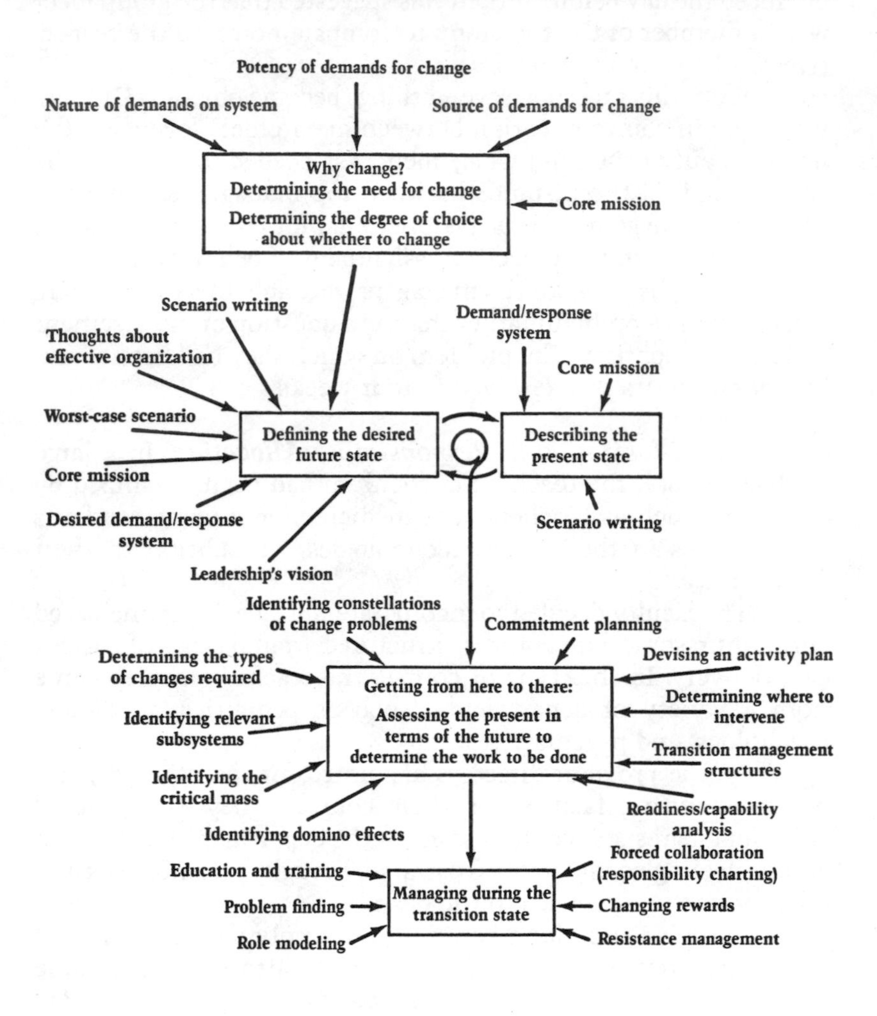

Figure 9–3
The Change Management Process

problems create role confusion about who should do what to whom, traditional methods such as more specific job descriptions, mediation by the boss, or separating the protagonists tend to be unsatisfactory. A process that allows participants in a complex interface to sit down together and determine their optimal behavior in different classes of tasks tends to produce positive change and increase satisfaction. Responsibility charting is one method that has had a number of effective applications in dealing with this issue.

Summary

We have looked at the commitment planning process; what is involved in getting commitment, how to develop a commitment chart, and a series of strategies for getting commitment. These strategies include problem finding, educational intervention, resistance management, role modeling, changing reward systems, and finally, "forced collaboration," with the specific application of responsibility charting.

In the process of change, particularly during the transition state, the strategies for managing the changing of the organization's work and for getting the commitment of the necessary people or groups go hand in hand. At this point, we have completed our review of the change process and the issues in managing it. Figure 9–3 offers a summary overview of the points we have described and illustrated throughout this book. We would readily admit that the steps outlined in the diagram are, to be sure, an oversimplification of the very complex process required for effective management of organizational change. We have tried to provide some sense of order — if you will, organizing principles — to guide managerial thinking and actions taken to cope with the complexity of contemporary organizational life and to face the challenges of managing change within turbulent and uncertain environments.

In the final chapter, we will take a look at what we see as some of the issues in change management facing organization leaders in the years ahead.

10

Managing Complexity

At the beginning of the book, we said that the dilemma all executive management faces is how to facilitate and manage change and development, on the one hand, and at the same time "keep the store running."

Managing change in complex organizations is like steering a sailboat in turbulent water and stormy winds. If you're on a course to some destination and the wind is blowing at gale force dead broadside, you have to make a number of critical choices. If you head into the wind, you'll lose speed and direction although you probably can ride out the storm. If you let the wind carry you too far, it might blow the boat over; and if you let it go a little less far than that, it may well drive you off course. If you decide to hold rigidly to your course at all costs, you may find that the winds rip the sails or even break off the mast.

The true sailor, knowing these choices, works *with* the wind. He or she will bring the boat up close between gusts, "fall off" a little on the next gust, and come back up to course in such a way that the boat stays on the compass heading toward its destination through many short-term decisions, which go with or against the prevailing winds in an appropriate combination.

This "feel" for steering an organization is the salient characteristic of the effective executive manager of change.

To "keep the course," several essentials must be provided:

- a clear destination, or *vision*
- landmarks, or *intermediate checkpoints*
- accurate, detailed maps, or *scenarios*
- a clear knowledge of the condition and capacity of the "boat" or the organization
- the ability to get the best performance out of the boat or organization

Let us leave the nautical metaphor at this point. What this all means is that organization leaders must understand the *organizational system* (formal structures plus relevant environment). Leaders must also, through their own behavior, demonstrate their own commitment to effectiveness, excellence, and improvement. They must be willing to invest in the training, relocation of decisions, and reorganization necessary to achieve their priorities. Operationally, these leaders must be ready to manage:

Changes — in the *environment*

Changes — in *organizational priorities:*
Market- vs. technology-driven
Quality vs. price priority

Changes — in *structures:*
From functional to business or matrix structure
Parallel structures and temporary systems

Changes — in the *ways work is done:*
People managing their own work
Inspection closer to work

Changes — in *personnel policies:*
Rewarding innovation and creativity along with production and stability

Changes — in *roles:*
Building more independent entrepreneurial groups within a large organization

Changes — in *culture:*
- Preparing to eliminate traditions
- Reexamining current beliefs, assumptions, norms, and customs
- Explicitly espousing core values.

Managing complexity involves a strong ability to deal with ambiguity, a talent for managing conflicts, a deep concern for people and their potential, the ability to maintain a balance between reliance on systematic planning skills and gut feeling, and — most important — having a sense of vision.

The Art of Managing Change

Intervention in large systems is, and will probably continue to be, largely an art. But even an artist needs to have *some* technique and *some* tools, and experience in using them. The artist painting a canvas has extensively studied form, graphics, and color mixes, and relies on both experience and intuition to create the painting. The manager of the change process and the organization consultant who helps must both be judged on the "artistry" of their product. We have offered a few techniques, tools, and formulas to use as a base for these acts.

It is obvious that the process of intervention is complex. One of the biggest traps for large-system change efforts is the failure of organizational leaders to resist the temptation to rush through the planning process to get to the "action" stage. Although the pressures for immediate results often arise from a need to eliminate the acute negative consequences of the problem, it has been our experience that a great portion of large-system change efforts fail due to a lack of understanding on the part of the organizational leadership of what the process of intervention and change involves. When the manager lacks an appreciation for and understanding of the true complexity of the intervention process, it is predictable that the emphasis will be on "action" or results. Management must gain a basic understanding of the whats, hows, and whys of the change management process, and be able to recognize its developmental and interdependent nature, as a necessary condition for success in planned change efforts.

Successful intervention in large systems is becoming more of a science than an art, but it is still not a cookbook process, nor is it ever likely to be. However, the utilization of systematic procedures and technologies in the planning and management of large systems change can only be of help.

We hope that this book has helped those involved in managing change in complex organizations, especially top organizational leaders, to understand better the process of change or transition management and to have a clearer idea of what is required to facilitate and improve that process.